Nazi Steel

Nazi Steel

Friedrich Flick and German Expansion in Western Europe, 1940–1944

Marcus O. Jones

NAVAL INSTITUTE PRESS

ANNAPOLIS, MARYLAND

NAVAL INSTITUTE PRESS
291 Wood Road
Annapolis, MD 21402

Library of Congress Cataloging-in-Publication Data

Jones, Marcus O.
 Nazi steel : Friedrich Flick and German expansion in Western
Europe, 1940–1944 / Marcus O. Jones.
    p. cm.
 Includes bibliographical references and index.
 ISBN 978-1-59114-421-2 (hardcover : alk. paper) — ISBN 978-
1-61251-095-8 (e-book) 1. Flick, Friedrich, 1883–1972. 2. Flick,
Friedrich, 1883–1972—Political activity. 3. Industrialists—
Germany—Biography. 4. Steel industry and trade—Political
aspects—Germany—History—20th century. 5. World War,
1939–1945—Economic aspects—Germany. 6. Germany—Economic
policy—1933–1945. 7. Steel-works—France—Lorraine—History—
20th century. 8. World War, 1939–1945—Economic aspects—
France—Lorraine. 9. World War, 1939–1945—Occupied territories.
10. Germany—Territorial expansion—History—20th century. I.
Title.
 HC282.5.F54J66 2012
 338.7'669142092—dc23
                              2011047972

♾ This paper meets the requirements of ANSI/NISO z39.48-1992
(Permanence of Paper).
Printed in the United States of America.

20 19 18 17 16 15 14 13 12   9 8 7 6 5 4 3 2 1
First printing

Book layout and composition: Alcorn Publication Design

Contents

Introduction

This study explores an exemplary instance of the close interaction between private and official interests in planning and executing the programs of the Nazi government, namely the acquisition in 1941 of the Rombach steel works by the German industrialist Friedrich Flick. The industrial concern headed by Flick was among the largest and most influential steel producers and manufacturers of war matériel in the German economy during World War II.[1] Its activities in the occupied territories of Western Europe centered on control of the Rombach works, a large operation established in Lorraine in the late nineteenth century by German industrialists and expropriated by France, along with the entire region, in the aftermath of World War I. After successful military operations against France in 1940, the Nazi regime actively sought the collusion of the German industrial community in mobilizing the productive capacity of occupied territories for the war effort, and numerous private German businessmen advanced claims on the lucrative assets in Lorraine and adjacent regions. In his bid to gain control of the Rombach works, Flick was successful for reasons specific to his position within the Nazi German economic system and the character of his interests. This account of his activities, then, serves as a fine example of Nazi economic and occupation policy and its response to party, business, and bureaucratic influences.

Flick's campaign to gain the wartime trusteeship of the Rombach works suggests much about the relationship between the German industrial community and the Nazi regime, and their joint role in expropriating and using the industrial assets of occupied Europe. Prior historical research provides general points of departure for a survey of that relationship, having demonstrated that the Nazi regime could count on a substantial convergence of opinion among the leading members of Germany's traditional "conservative elites," especially about the desirability of a European continent restructured to Germany's advantage. In contrast to an uncomplicated "primacy of politics," wherein the ideological imperatives of the Nazi state alone straightforwardly defined the complexion of economic policy, the balance of scholarly opinion finds a commonality of general interest among economic and political authorities: "In a process of gradual accommodation, the conservative elites in the bureaucracy, military, industry, and academia increasingly passed into the Nazi camp, because here they anticipated the realization of their long-cherished foreign policy expectations."[2] While noteworthy ruptures between the regime and industrialists were apparent in other areas, especially after the regime consolidated its influence over the domestic economy in 1936 and made deep inroads into the autonomy of private industry, a broad consensus held that the iron ore and steel assets of Lorraine, constructed largely with German capital between 1878 and 1918, should serve after 1940 as the basis of an autarkic, export-oriented, and efficient German industry.[3]

That broad consensus should not obscure the differences that separated many industrialists from the regime over the form that incorporation of foreign assets should assume. Within the parameters established by the regime, there remained discretionary space for the largest German industrialists to define and pursue their interests in competition with one another and, to a certain extent, with the regime. The specific scope and character of that space in the case of an industrialist like Flick and the way he functioned within it have become more accessible to historical analysis with the end of the Cold War and the opening of new archives.[4] Consideration of it also draws necessarily on evolving conceptions of the Nazi German economy and the mobilization efforts it contained. Historians have long undertaken analyses of the Nazi economic system from a wide variety of perspectives, including theories of modernization, Marxist-Leninist doctrines of capitalist imperialism, and more straightforward appraisals of the relationship between ideological predispositions and policy outcomes.[5] Most notable for the purposes of this study is Alan Milward's seminal study of the French economy during the Nazi occupation of 1940–1944, which drew heavily on his earlier groundbreaking assessment of the economic basis of German operational doctrines.[6] Subsequent historiography has not been kind to Milward. In his early study, Milward argued that a lack of military demand, resulting from a number of factors, stunted the extent of German war mobilization before 1942. Guiding this interpretation was the presumption that Hitler sought in his war planning above all to avoid a decline in German civilian morale, which he and a broad swath of German officialdom blamed for Germany's defeat in World War I. Milward took the strategic corollary to this view to have been the doctrine of blitzkrieg warfare, which emphasized brief, decisive campaigns based on partial mobilization and directed toward the seizure of those resources required for the next advance. Building on this insight, Milward argued that Nazi policy in France, and by implication occupied Western Europe generally, derived broadly from the anticapitalist, reactionary socioeconomic goals of National Socialism. Although he concedes that Hitler himself never propounded a coherent vision of a future European economic order, Milward suggests that the ideas of Karl Haushofer, Werner Daitz, and other theorists of a putative European *Grossraumwirtschaft*, or integrated large-scale economy, steered the formulation of policy in occupied Western Europe. Such notions implied extension of the domestic German autarkic policies of the 1930s to the occupied territories and a willingness by the Nazis to disregard conventional market mechanisms, by which is presumably meant consumer-driven supply and demand. Furthermore, and more questionably, Milward argues that "economic policy in occupied France was conceived solely in terms of the Blitzkrieg economy," according to which comprehensive mobilization of the economy was undesirable out of fear of undermining the stability of the National Socialist regime.[7] With the reversal in Germany's strategic fortunes after 1942, the heightened production requirements of an intensified war effort ruled out the further pursuit of radical occupation measures to recast the shape of Europe. According to Milward, Nazi conceptions of European economic organization therefore were never realized.

There are two primary objections to the foregoing understanding of Nazi economic policies in occupied Europe. The first deals with the larger productive framework within which occupation policy was cast. Research on the German economy over the past three decades has demonstrated that the initial phase of partial mobilization, stretching from 1936 (at the earliest) or 1940 (at the latest) to early 1942, was less a component of a strategic doctrine to wage conventional war on a limited economic basis than the result of a failure to mobilize efficiently.[8] Of fundamental importance for the present study is the work of Rolf-Dieter Müller, who has explained the slackening of mobilization efforts after the French campaign of 1940 as reflecting a lack of appreciation among policymakers for the realistic economic requirements of Hitler's strategic intentions. Compounding the problem, moreover, was the practice among military procurement agencies of contracting with smaller, less efficient armaments producers to avoid the political and systemic pressures of a more thorough mobilization.[9] In a series of provocative articles, Richard Overy has demonstrated that the German economy was close to full mobilization in summer and autumn of 1940, or at least as close as the polycratic confusion of Nazi German administration allowed.[10] Detailed analyses of Nazi labor policy and public finance, civilian consumption and spending, and war output suggest that the Nazi regime anticipated and planned for a long war in 1938–39. The regime introduced the most important real and percentage increases in taxation and armaments spending in the opening years of the war, and considerable redirection of consumer industries toward military purposes accompanied an effort to organize the labor force, especially women, to an extent far greater than historians long appreciated. The profusion of self-duplicating military, civilian, and party agencies characteristic of the Nazi regime was more of an obstacle than stimulus to the efficient organization of the economy. Therefore, the stagnation of output in the early stages of the war detailed in the postwar United States Strategic Bombing Survey, the findings of which constitute the basis of most assessments of German economic performance, resulted not from a considered strategy but from mismanagement of the war economy on a massive scale.

The second objection deals with the presumptive link between the ideological predispositions of the authorities and the policy outcomes pursued. Many of the economic measures cited by historians as characteristically National Socialist need not necessarily have derived from Nazi economic ideas, such as they were.[11] Autarkic policies on a continental scale can be viewed as a strategic necessity, pursued by the regime to counteract the vulnerabilities of dependence on overseas sources of raw materials. The Nazi regime's willingness to aid private German interests like Friedrich

Flick's concern in subduing European rivals and securing market share and assets in the occupied territories hardly seems practically different from French attempts to overturn German dominance of certain market segments in the wake of World War I, even if it was justified by different ideological arguments.[12]

This is not to suggest that the Nazi regime pursued an agenda, however well or poorly, akin to those of other nation-states in wartime. Rather, in considering Nazi plans and policies one must be mindful of a key characteristic of the regime, namely the extent to which it succeeded in harnessing apparently rational means to the pursuit of murderously irrational ends. Thus, some historians have interpreted the proliferation of Nazi economic offices and authorities, which in many cases gave party hacks priority over technical functionaries, more as a makeshift for maintaining the dictatorship than a program of radical economic organization.[13] In other words, certain features of the Nazi economic program in the occupied West appear consistent with the predictable imperatives of wartime mobilization, whereas others, such as the wholesale deportation or extermination of ethnic minorities, were clearly not. In the absence of an integrated history of German economic and occupation policy in Western Europe, therefore, overarching reliance on the idea of a distinctive Nazi New Order to account for economic policy seems questionable.

Basic to the economic potential of the Nazi regime to carry out its program of conquest and exploitation in Europe was the German corporate community, which even in late 1939 owned and managed the overwhelming bulk of German production. Without the collusion of German managers and private businessmen, the Nazi regime stood no chance of providing successfully for a war to secure vast new areas for a future German empire and reshape the ethnic face of Europe through what one prominent historian has referred to as a "demographic revolution."[14] For that reason, the study of German corporations during the Nazi period has recently enjoyed a resurgence nothing short of remarkable.[15] Over the past twenty years scholarship has advanced well beyond the broad and unsustainable claims, common in the postwar period, of hegemonic corporate control of the Nazi political leadership.[16] It has been demonstrated definitively, for example, that the German corporate elite was not primarily or directly responsible for the Nazi seizure of power in January 1933.[17] To the extent that one can speak of a coherent program, corporate political activities centered on situating the Nazi Party in a context of antisocialist and, to some extent, antidemocratic conservative reactions to the crisis of the Weimar Republic. However, like much of German society, the industrial community adapted quickly to the changed political circumstances after Hitler's appointment as chancellor in 1933 and moved to consolidate its own position within the corporatized Nazi state. "Neither cooperation nor resistance is the answer," as the *Reichsverband der deutschen Industrie* put it in 1933, "but compulsory adaptation."[18] Seen in this light, the degree of collaboration with the regime among German businessmen in the twelve-year history of the Third Reich varied in ways little different from that apparent in other social constituencies throughout the country. Their actions and decisions had much to do with the industry in which they worked, their individual backgrounds and religious sentiments, and the regions in which they lived. There can be no doubt, of course, that opportunism and readiness to cooperate with the authorities was much in evidence among businessmen. Few actively resisted the Nazi regime, so few that a greater historiographical problem is presented by deviations from a standard range of business reactions to the regime than by conformity.[19]

Historians in the 1980s and 1990s undertook a series of informative studies depicting the economic life of German corporations under what were anomalously capitalistic circumstances at best.[20] Since then the field has exploded, with scholars on both sides of the Atlantic producing searching new studies of numerous firms and industrial sectors. In privileging historical detail over generalization, historians have heeded Alan Milward's 1974 assertion that the "most vital field of future research must be to explore the history of particular industries and even particular firms."[21] The numerous and resulting microstudies, of which the present effort is one, have presented a complex picture of interwoven state and private economic activities and interests, in which the former used the latter to secure the ends required for its racial and military program of conquest, and the latter used the former to pursue secular ends of economic gain and social empowerment. The outcome of the relationship did not reflect well on the putative "economic logic" of private entrepreneurship, according to which one can explain almost any measure, however unscrupulous, by the probable financial gains or the enhanced security of one's narrow interests. In the wake of the Holocaust and the complicity of otherwise ordinary businessmen in some of the Nazi regime's most heinous activities, such as the Aryanization campaign of the 1930s to divest Jewish businessmen of their property, few today would doubt that conscientious economic activity involves at least a minimal degree of ethical conduct.[22]

Assessing the activities of an industrial concern in the Nazi period, as is true of virtually any social or economic institution in the modern world, demands multiple perspectives. Insights gleaned from economics, organizational theory, sociology, and institutional analysis all have strong claims on the interpretive thrust of business history and influence the shape of our historical understanding. This is partly due to the fact that the basic hierarchical structures in question, the early twentieth-century German corporation and the highly developed market economy of a large western nation, are dauntingly complex in their diversity, scale, and internal organization, to say nothing of the motives and backgrounds of the persons inhabiting them.[23] Decision-making in such organizations and the impersonal bureaucratic logic that sometimes appears to govern it also complicate the historian's task of assessing causality and assigning responsibility. The basic lack of familiarity with the internal practices and processes of large commercial enterprises apparent among most academic historians who wrestle with the decisions of prominent German industrial figures, moreover, renders the resulting assessments somewhat less convincing.[24]

Friedrich Flick's personal ownership of the different operations within his concern somewhat lessens the interpretive difficulty of accounting for its activities and objectives. In contrast to most industrial enterprises in Nazi Germany, which were publicly held and collectively managed, Flick incurred responsibility for what took place within the many subunits of his industrial empire to the extent to which he exercised control and reaped the benefits. Recognition of the corporate legal status of the individuals on top, however, in no way lessens the analytic difficulty inherent in studying such complex and diverse operations. The sprawling character of his concern forced Flick to delegate substantial responsibility to subordinates throughout the Nazi period and especially during the war, when the tempo of developments and the abnormal business environment demanded more rapid and localized responses to problems. The way in which his subordinates reacted to events and shaped the larger issues with which Flick himself eventually dealt is not always clear from the evidence. All the same, a historical reconstruction of Flick's motives and decisions under the Nazi regime helps to shed light on the nature of his responsibility for what happened in Europe during the Third Reich and on how an instrument as amoral as a business entity, based as it is on rational calculations of interest, became a pliable tool in the hands of a destructive regime.

The first chapter of this study details Nazi views of Lorraine and its place in the world view of Hitler especially. The study of Lorraine figures only sporadically in postwar assessments of Nazi occupation and economic policy, and few historians have considered its role in the strategic ambitions of the German nation between 1871 and 1945.[25] Consequently, historians have little understanding of the specific manner whereby the Nazi regime occupied and administered the economic resources of the region. The second chapter explores the career and background of Friedrich Flick before and during the first seven years of Nazi rule, as he drew closer to the Nazi leadership, if not its ideological program, and participated in the fulfillment of its agenda, especially the economic disenfranchisement of the Jews. The second chapter also provides a preliminary perspective on the position of industry in the Nazi state, important to the motivation of a steel industrialist like Flick for expanding into Lorraine in 1940. The economic significance of Lorraine for the German steel industry before the war is developed in the third chapter along with a discussion of its historical background. Flick's campaign to acquire the Rombach works is the subject of the fourth chapter, followed by a review of his attempts to negotiate more favorable terms for his trusteeship after 1941. Finally, the fifth chapter looks at the effect of the incorporation of Lorraine on German iron ore supply and steel production, and examines why Flick's trusteeship of the Rombach works proved a failure.

Chapter 1

Nazi German Plans and Policies in Lorraine

dolf Hitler's writings and comments on Western Europe and Alsace-Lorraine and early wartime measures to administer the region laid the basis of the economic and industrial framework within which German seizures of French industrial assets took place.[1] The secondary importance of Alsace-Lorraine in Hitler's strategic conception and the disjointed character of Nazi governance in general made certain that no coherent program for assimilating the resources and assets in the region existed prior to the Nazi German takeover. Occupation, administration, and eventually economic incorporation into the Reich proceeded on an improvised basis and as a result of maneuvering by state, party, and economic interest groups. The economic circumstances of the German war effort in 1940, especially the severe bottlenecks in the steel industry and desire of the authorities to exploit Lorraine's valuable economic assets for the war effort as quickly as possible, all contributed to Friedrich Flick's prospects for expanding the reach of his conglomerate. Nazi planners viewed the industrial assets of eastern France as a crucial complement to their overtaxed armaments industry and moved quickly to assert control over them, granting broad concessions to private industry in the expectation that it would manage the assets in a fashion advantageous to the war economy.

In planning and executing policy throughout occupied Europe, Hitler sought not the moderate reshaping of national boundaries envisioned by Weimar revisionists, but a radical alteration of all existing frontiers and ethnic arrangements. Although his ideas neither assumed a systematic form nor responded in obvious ways to external circumstances, certain basic outlines are clear. As late as the autumn of 1941, Hitler entertained a vague notion of a Greater Germanic Empire organized on a racial basis, stretching from Scandinavia to the Alps and from the Atlantic to the Ural Mountains, in which the Germans would launch a great Nordic settlement drive to the East.[2] He evidently held that the territorial and racial restructuring of the continent—effected through annexations, forced labor, and the regime's pitiless racial policy—would lay the foundation for National Socialist claims to world power status and an inevitable showdown with the last great rival across the Atlantic. However, he never formulated, or chose not to reveal, the specific scope of the eventual New Order in Europe and his intentions toward managing it.[3] His inclination to postpone fundamental decisions on occupation policy until the end of the war ensured that improvised decisions and contradictory solutions to administrative and economic problems abounded—there was "neither a coordination of leadership committees nor a balanced planning of the overall war effort."[4] Nevertheless, his programmatic statements and diplomatic gestures in the 1920s and early 1930s reveal important features of the hypothetical Nazi New Order, most prominently in the case of the Eastern territories but in the West as well.

Any account of Nazi plans and intentions in Western Europe must recognize at the outset that region's secondary importance in Hitler's plans, particularly in the more developed form they assumed by the 1930s.[5] Hitler viewed the Nordic countries as racially akin to Germany and unworthy of serious attention until strategic considerations in 1940, namely the possibility of an Allied initiative in the region, dictated the need to occupy Norway and Denmark. The German administration in those countries, while certainly unpleasant, was remarkably gentle relative to that imposed elsewhere in Europe.[6] Hitler and other Nazi officials retained a similarly benign view of the Dutch and Flemish peoples of the Low Countries, whose strategic impotence relative to their English and French neighbors forced them, in Hitler's mind, into the enemy camp. Their chief importance prior to the war lay in the prospect of German access to the French north and a means of bypassing the Maginot Line of defense along the French eastern frontier. After 1940, direct and accountable trade continued to flow between Germany and the Western European nations, albeit in a manner beneficial to Germany.[7]

As regards the French, Hitler's early foreign-policy ideas were fixated on a war of revenge, almost certainly because of his immediate memories of World War I. In 1920, he said, "Our enemy is across the Rhine, not in Italy or elsewhere."[8] A campaign to undo the Versailles settlement and end French hegemony on the European continent appeared as Hitler's principal short-term objective in the absence of the more openly articulated ideas of territorial expansion that were to come later.[9] Reactive notions of revenge coexisted awkwardly with his other, proactive foreign-policy priorities, namely the creation of a German sphere of power invulnerable to traditional enemies. If Germans were to gain the territory essential to their continued survival, Hitler came to believe, it would have to come at the expense of Russia and the states of Eastern Europe. By the late 1920s, Hitler had refined his foreign-policy plans into a clear preference for eastward expansion. His ideas by that point had come to focus no longer primarily on revision of Versailles; revenge against France, while still expedient and desirable, assumed a significance more strategic than fundamental—that of eliminating the most dangerous military threat to Germany's ability to wage war against the Soviet Union.[10] French ambitions to dominate the European continent would always be a question of life and death for Germany, Hitler finally asserted, but the country nevertheless had more urgent concerns elsewhere.[11]

Alsace and Lorraine figured scarcely at all in Hitler's public statements during the 1920s and 1930s, and appear only to a minimal extent in surviving records of the secret communications between Hitler and German policy elites during the 1930s.[12] The two provinces, acquired by Germany in the Franco-Prussian War of 1870–71 and lost again in the Versailles settlement after World War I, represented an issue of minor importance within Hitler's overall approach to relations with the Western allies. Hitler assumed in *Mein Kampf* that a successful war against France would result not only in a substantial revision of Germany's western borders, but more important, would serve as the strategic foundation for his Eastern campaign.[13] His unpublished second book, completed in 1928, expanded on this basic concept: "A German victory over France with Italian help will bring us Alsace-Lorraine at the least and at most the freedom to implement a really generous policy of expansion. And from that alone can Germany live long in the future."[14] Viewed from that perspective, it is unsurprising that Alsace-Lorraine warranted but a handful of minor digressions in his writings. Aside from criticism of Bismarck's unsatisfactory "Reichsland-Solution" to the question of the territories, Hitler remarked in *Mein Kampf* simply that France had stolen Alsace-Lorraine, thereby implying that it rightfully belonged to Germany regardless of how it factored into his larger strategic intentions.[15] However, the incidental character of his remarks need not imply that Hitler dismissed the area as unworthy of his attention, merely that he considered other priorities more vital. According to Hermann Rauschning, he indicated in the summer of 1932 that Germany would never abandon claims to Alsace-Lorraine, less as a result of its ethnic German heritage than because the region was essential to the coherence of a powerful future German nation.[16] Hitler likely regarded a revision of the status of Alsace-Lorraine in the event of a victory over France as so obvious as not to require elaborate justification.[17]

The need to consolidate German public opinion in the event of his successful attainment of political power and allay western, particularly French, apprehensions toward his future intentions gave Hitler grounds to moderate his approach to questions of western border revision in the early 1930s. Accordingly, historians have drawn attention to what they perceive as a cynical shift in Hitler's foreign-policy articulations after 1931.[18] France, as the strongest military power on the continent, figured only as a risk factor inhibiting action against the Soviet Union. The early, wary French reactions to Hitler's appointment as chancellor in January 1933 betrayed little indication of the accommodation for which Hitler might have hoped in moderating his approach to border revision, however implacably he viewed French animosity. For his part, Hitler had begun to question whether he would need to defeat France before undertaking his crusade against the Soviet Union, believing that fears of renewed European conflict would force France to adopt a compliant line.[19] Indeed, he downplayed his formerly strident rhetoric to such an extent that some observers thought he had altogether renounced his revisionist program of the *Kampfzeit*.[20] He widely trumpeted his desire for a peaceful European order predicated on parity between the powers, particularly in communications with the French.

Renunciations of any claim to Alsace and Lorraine increasingly became a motif in his relations with the French. He assured the French ambassador in Berlin as early as September 1933 that he no longer demanded the return of Alsace to the Reich.[21] In his March 1936 address to the Reichstag on the occasion of the German reoccupation of the Rhineland, Hitler proclaimed that after having labored "to slowly but surely establish the prerequisites for a German-French understanding," he had "removed from the German press all animosity against the French people." Most importantly for his intentions toward France, he had "removed the question of the everlasting revision of European borders from the atmosphere of public discussion in Germany."[22] As late as the Party Congress in September 1938, on the verge of his decisive reckoning with Czechoslovakia, Hitler considered the long-standing question of Alsace-Lorraine in the context of German relations with France and disavowed all further demands for revision, "because we [have] willed an end to this constant argument with France once and for all."[23] Shortly thereafter, in his speech at the Berlin Sportpalast on 26 September 1938, at the end of the Czechoslovak crisis, he reiterated that the "question of Alsace-Lorraine no longer exist[s] as far as we are concerned. It is a border area. . . . It is our impression that the inhabitants of the area would be the most happy if all the fighting about them ended. We do not wish for war with France. We want nothing of France! Nothing at all!"[24] Hitler's adamant renunciations of any revisionist demands and expressions of a desire for peace culminated in a joint declaration of both governments, initialed in Paris on 6 December 1938 by German foreign minister Joachim von Ribbentrop and French foreign minister Georges Bonnet. It acknowledged "that between their countries no questions of a territorial nature are outstanding and solemnly recognize as final the frontier between their countries as it now exists."[25] Finally, in his noon speech on 28 April 1939, Hitler sought to portray his policy toward France in the most conciliatory light possible. While struggling to justify the incorporation into Nazi Germany of virtually the entire ethnic Czech population, Hitler declared that he had "not, as France did in the years 1870–71, referred to the cession of Alsace–Lorraine as intolerable in the future. No, I carefully differentiated between the Saar territory and the two other former Reichsländer. And I have not revised my stance on the matter, nor will I revise it in the future."[26] From his instrumental use of the issue in his diplomatic maneuverings during the 1930s, it seems clear that Alsace-Lorraine was never an absolute objective in Hitler's program of conquest. Far from adhering to an inflexible principle of German ethnic consolidation in Europe, Hitler used the standing of the former German territories as a means of alternately assuaging the French and demonstrating his progressive intentions toward the other European nations.

As he prepared to invade Poland on 1 September 1939, Hitler seized upon the issue of Alsace-Lorraine in an effort to head off imminent Western military intervention in the first of his wars. In a note to French Minister-President Daladier on 27 August, Hitler referred to the "voluntary limitation of German demands for existence in the West" as a means of eliminating any basis for Franco-German conflict: "The German people have thereby renounced two provinces, which once belonged to the old German Empire, were conquered through a massive bloodletting, and finally with much more blood defended. This renunciation represents not a tactical stance for the benefit of the outside world, but a resolution whose logical substantiation is evidenced in all of our actions."[27] Even after the English and French declarations of war, Hitler offered peace to both powers in a Reichstag address of 6 October 1939 on the basis of German expansion in the East, a return of former German colonies, and a maintenance of the status quo in the West. Hitler crowned his extension of the last condition by boasting that "I have declined even to bring up the question of Alsace-Lorraine, not because I was forced to do so, but because the affair is not a problem which should trouble French-German relations. I accepted the 1919 settlement. I declined to let a problem drive us into bloody war, a question which stands in no relation to Germany's vital interests. The only thing it is fit for is to plunge every other generation into a renewed fruitless war."[28]

His public pronouncements notwithstanding, Hitler remained firm in his intention to smash French military power as a prelude to his program of eastern expansion.[29] No reference to Alsace-Lorraine is apparent in his deliberations at this stage, as was so frequently the case in his statements regarding France prior to 1933, but he almost certainly did not have in mind any repetition of Bismarck's misbegotten Reichsland solution, by which a special administrative status had the effect of exacerbating a sense of separateness among the region's inhabitants. Hitler would seek to ensure both that France was prostrate before Nazi power and that the people of Alsace-Lorraine would be integrated into the Reich.

With the rapid pace and great magnitude of the military situation in the West foremost in their minds, neither Hitler nor other Nazi Party planners conceived in advance the specific form measures regarding a reorganized Alsace-Lorraine should assume. The unexpectedly swift annihilation of French forces forced the new French government of Marshall Philippe Petain to seek an armistice much sooner than most thought likely.[30] On the evening of 22 June 1940, French and German negotiators met in the historic railway wagon of Marshall Foch in the Compiègne Forest and signed an armistice to take effect on 25 June.[31] The armistice contained no specific provisions on the fate of Alsace-Lorraine, whose status throughout negotiations remained unclear and subject to later determination, a point of awkward uncertainty for the French.[32] Indeed, as the race to acquire the industrial assets in the region heated up, the German foreign office, ever the stickler for international legal niceties, sought to dampen enthusiasm for the effort, claiming that until a peace treaty stipulated the final status of the Lorraine, the industrial assets there could not be legitimately viewed as enemy property and hence subject to expropriation.[33]

The failure to address the question of Alsace-Lorraine's future legal status in no way implied an abandonment of German claims to the territories; rather, it left matters sufficiently open-ended that those with axes to grind could begin to vie for position. This included, among others, the head of the Presidial Chancellery, Otto Meissner, an Alsatian by birth, who far into 1940 entertained notions of becoming a Protektor, a sort of regional potentate, of a unified Alsace-Lorraine encompassing parts of Luxemburg as well.[34] He was disappointed, however, when Hitler finally made public in mid-1940 his determination to dissolve the administrative unity of the region and appoint chiefs of civil administration for each of the two territories. In Alsace, the task fell to Robert Wagner, the Gauleiter of Baden, while Josef Bürckel, Gauleiter of the Saar-Pfalz, took up the reins of administration in Lorraine.[35] Bürckel was among the least savory characters in a regime full of disreputable types. A veteran of World War I and a primary-school teacher for much of the interwar period, he joined the Nazi Party in 1925 and within a year became Gauleiter of the Rheinpfalz. During the 1935 plebiscite to determine the fate of the Saarland, he had defamed those opposed to the reincorporation of that region into Germany as traitors to the fatherland and advocated the use of terrorism against them. Hitler had tapped him once before to oversee the absorption of a region into the Nazi orbit by appointing Bürckel Gauleiter of Vienna in April 1938. In light of this background, Hitler had ample reason to consider Bürckel fit to administer a subjugated territory in a manner consistent with the brutal dictates of the Nazi policy.[36]

Historical research, especially in the form of localized studies, has done much to demonstrate the importance of Gau leadership in Nazi Germany for bringing the economy into line with the ideological and military ambitions of the regime.[37] The local fusion of economic organs of the Nazi Party, state agencies, and private economic groups represented a characteristically heterogeneous and surprisingly effective mix of organizational polycracy and the Nazi leadership principle (*Führerprinzip*). Gau leadership cadres worked to politicize the population through outright propaganda, social engineering on a greater or lesser scale, and domestic infiltration, and thus were very much on the front lines of local efforts to bring a Nazi face to public administration.[38] The Aryanization campaigns of the 1930s to purge Jews from German economic life owed much to the local initiatives of the Gauwirtschaftsapparat, although the specific roles of those agencies varied between regions.[39]

The effectiveness of Gau administration notwithstanding, the absence of a clear policy regarding the political or economic future of Alsace-Lorraine was a major liability as Bürckel assumed his position as chief of the civil administration for Lorraine under the Army High Command shortly after the beginning of the offensive in the West. As a result, Bürckel's administration unfolded more in response to short-term circumstances than as a well-considered and efficient plan. For the army, the appointment of a civil administrator tasked with liaison work with regional civilian agencies, subordinate to the military high command, was a normal part of the administration of a conquered region.[40] Nominally, the civil administrator was obliged to defer to the authority of the Wehrmacht High Command in disputed matters. Bürckel, however, viewed himself from the outset as a direct representative of the Führer, with all of the responsibilities and latitude such a role implied. On 15 June 1940 he wrote to Hitler detailing his ideas regarding the incorporation of Alsace-Lorraine into the Reich and proposed his own appointment as "Reichskommissar" in Lorraine, a position similar to what he had held in Austria after the Anschluß in 1938. That would bring him broad authority to mold affairs in direct negotiation with anyone and without deference to the Wehrmacht.[41] Four days later, a proposal of the military administration foresaw the establishment of a civilian administration divorced from military control and suggested those Nazi officials already attached to the military commands, Wagner and Bürckel, to head them.[42] Such a step clearly implied an attempt to return the areas to some form of administrative "normalcy" and expedite the process of de facto annexation. As Göring put it that same day, "Alsace-Lorraine will be reincorporated into the Reich."[43]

For short-term administrative purposes, Hitler consented to the reestablishment of the old administrative division between Alsace and Lorraine, which quickly led to the erection of a customs border between the two.[44] On 1 July, Hans Lammers, the head of the Reich Chancellery, contacted State Secretary Stuckart in the Interior Ministry and indicated that Hitler was considering the final incorporation of Alsace-Lorraine by proclamation, possibly in a speech to the Reichstag to take place within a week.[45] The Führer nevertheless wavered. At the Reichstag session of 19 July, for instance, Alsace-Lorraine was not even mentioned. Shortly thereafter, Gauleiter Wagner reported "in the strictest confidence" to his chief adviser, Robert Ernst, that the Führer had intimated that the incorporation of Alsace-Lorraine would be eventually effected by means of a secret treaty between Germany and France.[46] Historians have not uncovered any plans for a formal union, but it seems clear that Hitler had resolved to bring the territories into the Reich as regions on a par with their German neighbors. For all political and economic purposes, this meant, in the words of a senior Reich official, that "[a]lthough the constitutional annexation has not yet taken place, Alsace and Lorraine should be managed as though it has."[47] Further evidence that the region would be considered part of the Reich regardless of its international legal status is provided by the quasi-official journal *Neues Staatsrecht*, which by 1943 could claim that "[a]fter the military reconquest, so far as administration was concerned, Alsace and Lorraine were reincorporated into the Reich. An incorporation of the territory based on international law has not yet been effected. . . . The Reich has, however, made it apparent that it regards the re-occupation of Alsace and Lorraine . . . part of the final order of the future."[48]

Bürckel hardly required such official niceties. His chief concern was to widen his discretionary authority in Lorraine as much as possible. However, the same organizational incoherence that provided him with relative autonomy in running the affairs of his domain militated to some extent against his imposing his authority effectively and without regard to other parties. The "Führer Decree on the Provisional Administration in Alsace and Lorraine" of 2 August 1940 assigned the new administrations authority over civil matters and made them immediately subordinate to the Führer. The Army Command was confined to matters deemed of critical importance to military jurisdiction, a provision that actually left great discretion to the token army administration in Lorraine.[49] The civil administrators themselves were to attend to the reconstruction of the regions in accordance with general guidelines from Hitler and the technical directives of the highest Reich authorities. The Reich Minister of the Interior was assigned the task of acting as a central clearinghouse for a unified coordination of the different governmental agencies and civil administrators. The Interior Minister also retained the right, along with the Wehrmacht Supreme Command, to issue directives consistent with the implementation of the Führer's instructions.

By establishing dual spheres of civil and military authority without defining clearly the means of arbitrating between them, the first attempt to rationalize the administration of the new territories created as many problems as it solved. On 18 October 1940 Hitler signed a "Second Führer Decree" in which he further demarcated the civilian and military spheres and provided a firmer basis for the authority of the administrators. The civil administrators were to cooperate closely with the highest Reich authorities, but were to receive their instructions exclusively from Hitler, with one crucial exception: "As the German war economy requires unified planning also for Alsace and Lorraine . . . Reichsmarschall Göring can also issue directives to the Chiefs of Civil Administration in the context of those responsibilities incumbent upon him as Representative of the Four-Year Plan."[50] As events would show, this would place Göring in a position to make the final decision as to the disposition of industrial resources in the years after 1940.

It was in this crucible of unplanned and gradually evolving measures that German economic and industrial policy developed and the practical exploitation of Lorraine began. In anticipation, planning of a general nature had been undertaken in the late 1930s to ensure that the political and strategic imperatives of the Nazi state would define economic expansion in Europe. Lip service had long been paid to the notion that the thoroughgoing mobilization of the German economy for a massive war of attrition and conquest on the eastern front necessitated a ruthless exploitation of the industry of conquered and annexed territories. Göring, as Representative for the Four-Year Plan, underscored in secret guidelines of 2 August 1940 the necessity of acquiring the most critical industrial assets of occupied Europe at the earliest possible date: "The extension of the German influence over foreign enterprises is an objective of German political economy. It is not yet possible to determine whether and to what extent the peace treaty will effect the surrender of shares. It is now, however, that every opportunity should be used for the German economy, in time of war, to obtain access to material of interest to the economy in occupied territories and to prevent removals that might hinder the realization of the abovementioned aim."[51]

As is already evident to some extent here, the impetus behind the industrial expansion that took place after 1940 did not originate in commercial motives. To be sure, large German corporations saw great potential in the vast ore fields and processing mills of Lorraine and put forth proposals to demonstrate the desirability of reasserting German claims over them. But the real stimulus to industrial expansion lay in the war launched by the Nazi regime and the regime's firm control over the affairs of the conquered territories. The Nazi regime was forced by circumstances to rely upon private corporate initiative and expertise to fold the assets of occupied Europe into the war effort. It did not trust and could not necessarily rely upon private industry to act in a manner consistent with the best interests of the war economy at the pace and in the manner required by the Nazi regime's priorities. In constructing a large economic bloc in Central Europe to support a major war effort, the regime therefore took steps to ensure that political dictates or racial considerations assumed precedence over crass interest-seeking on the part of private industry.

The resolve of the regime to retain control over the economic affairs of Lorraine originated in a long-standing Nazi antipathy to big business. Nazism drew on a tradition of German economic thought that emphasized the primacy of the state in determining the means and ends by which productive human activity should be oriented, with a corresponding suspicion of unbridled capitalist competition.[52] Although a crude Social Darwinism defined much of Hitler's racial and social thinking, a fact which seemed to imply admiration for those who flourished under competitive circumstances, he remained leery of the bourgeoisie whom capitalism had elevated in social prominence and expressed hostility toward all but a handful of figures in the world of industry.[53] That such views resonated in the broader Nazi movement was apparent in party publications in March 1931 and June 1932 that described measures to direct private economic activity on behalf of the state.[54] While Hitler found it expedient to suppress such publications in the interest of mollifying the German business community, they reflected the essentially instrumental view of the Nazi party toward the economy and corporate world: "[T]heir common thrust was to cut the economy off from international influences, to increase government control over the factors of production, and to make the rights of ownership contingent on their exercise as the state sanctioned—to create, in short, an environment in which the institution of private property was never abandoned but the disposition and possession of it were always in question."[55]

The Nazi regime asserted its priorities forcefully at the time of the German takeover of Austrian industry in 1938. The regime permitted two German industrial firms, Krupp and the Vereinignte Stahlwerke (United Steel Works—VSt), to increase their participation in key Austrian enterprises, but only in a manner approved by the authorities.[56] The Austrian economy, Göring proclaimed, must be kept "firmly in the hands of the state."[57] A similar pattern of Nazi control guided economic expansion into Czechoslovakia, where government economic organs secured controlling shares in such leading concerns as Skoda and the Alpine Montangesellschaft. The state-sponsored Reichswerke Hermann Göring was far and away the most pervasive of the entities seeking to exert control over the resources of occupied countries, coming to dominate some two-thirds of the combined heavy industry in Austria and Czechoslovakia alone.[58] The onset of war in 1939 intensified what had already become a tendency on the part of official organs not merely to guide, but to control the economic expansion of German corporations in the interest of the war effort. A month after the invasion of Poland, Göring emphasized that the aim of German policy was the "reconstruction and expansion of the economy" and that the "safeguarding of [the productive facilities and supplies in the occupied territories] must be aimed at, as well as a complete incorporation into the Greater German economic system at the earliest possible time."[59]

The Nazi authorities constructed an elaborate command organization to govern the exploitation of the iron and steel resources of occupied Western Europe. Early on, Göring's Reichswerke organization assumed the most critical positions within the new system. On 5 July 1940 the Economics Ministry consented to the appointment of Paul Raabe, a director of the Reichswerke, as General Plenipotentiary for the mining and distribution of iron ore in Luxemburg and Lorraine (which included Longwy, Briey, Metz-Thionville, and Nancy).[60] His charge was to bring about a resumption and increase of ore production in the newly acquired territories, a job that would require not a little political discretion and subtlety.[61] Raabe's control over the ore mines, which defined the region's value both to the war economy and private steel industry, represented a major form of potential influence in the national economy.

Raabe was nominally bound by the directives of the Economics Ministry and the military administration in the occupied territories; historians have interpreted his appointment as characteristic of the control exerted over the exploitation of the occupied territories by Nazi economic authorities, particularly those of the expanding state productive apparatus.[62] However, note that attempts to delineate cleanly between state and private industrial interests in this context, to structure interpretations around a dichotomy based on clearly divergent interests and ambitions, must remain accommodating enough to account for the delicate interdependencies between the two. This is especially evident in the appointments on 1 July 1940 of Hermann Röchling, the most prominent industrialist of the Saar region, to the position of General Plenipotentiary for the Iron and Steel Industries in Lorraine, Meurthe-Moselle, and Longwy. He promptly began assigning German managers to operate firms abandoned by their French owners on a temporary basis. In doing so he elaborated guidelines to smooth the process of transitioning to German war production, providing for an ongoing freeze of wages at prewar levels, an inventory of materials and resources, and establishing a chain of authority through which problems involving the plants would be handled.[63] An Economics Ministry official responsible for the iron and steel industry, acting on behalf of Göring, also appointed Otto Steinbrinck as the plenipotentiary for the industries of Luxemburg, Belgium, and northern France. The latter had served as Friedrich Flick's chief deputy until December 1939, when personal differences between the two provoked Steinbrinck's departure. The economic fiefdoms of Röchling and Steinbrinck were eventually dissolved in June 1942, when their offices were subsumed within the new umbrella organization of the Reichsvereinigung Eisen.[64]

The form of German control over specific economic assets in occupied territories depended on the character of the asset and that of the German occupation in the region more generally.[65] The most extreme form of influence consisted in the outright replacement of the legally constituted corporate governance with a German administrator selected by the occupation authorities, so-called acting administrators or trustees.[66] However, for obvious reasons, the implementation of such drastic measures was impractical in the first months of the occupation, as the new German administrators sought to consolidate their power and prevent the predictable dislocation of defeat from deteriorating into complete chaos.

Initially, economic affairs in Lorraine proceeded along the same lines as applied to the remainder of occupied Europe. Consistent with its position as the leading edge of German influence in the occupied territories, the German army established on 23 June 1940 an early general basis for the appointment of temporary administrators for enterprises in the occupied West.[67] In the absence of more specific information pertaining to the financial health or productive capacities of most companies, the decree was necessarily vague regarding the privileges and responsibilities of the Germans tasked with superintending the firms. The appointment of a civil administrator by Hitler represented a strong shift in Lorraine away from central control toward a more local, Gau-oriented management of economic affairs, in a manner consistent with the region's de facto character as an integral part of the Reich. As the newly appointed head of the civil administration in Lorraine, Bürckel promptly issued on 27 July 1940 a supplemental order reserving for himself the rights to appoint all new industrial managers in Lorraine, review those appointments already made, and make decisions regarding future policies of any economic consequence.[68] Having asserted his authority over that of the army and any other organ in the region, Bürckel felt free to stake out even more sweeping powers in the economy of Lorraine. Not before late 1941, however, did Bürckel finally issue a series of decrees clarifying which enterprises were subject to sequestration by the German authorities, a category intended chiefly for those belonging to Jews or French persons lacking a residence in Lorraine.[69] Further decrees in 1942 obliged French shareholders to report the extent of their holdings in a given firm within a prescribed period or risk forfeiture. The measure served effectively to divest many French shareholders of their investments in enterprises, as such reporting was frequently impossible under wartime circumstances.[70] In essence, Bürckel's measures sought to establish a quasi-legal pretext for the future expropriation of the French industrial firms central to German war planning and production. His decision to retain the army's original policy of opening the economic field to German trustees from private firms had far-reaching implications both for the prospects of the war effort and for the problematic character of the industry-state relations that underpinned it.

Chapter 2

Friedrich Flick and His Activities under the Nazi Regime before 1940

B y the time of the Nazi seizure of power in January 1933, Friedrich Flick oversaw a business empire encompassing several steel and coal production and processing facilities throughout central Germany. The years of rearmament and expansion between 1933 and 1939 witnessed the incorporation into the Flick concern of the Hochofenwerk Lübeck, a major pig-iron processing plant, and several extensive mine operations belonging to the Petschek family. The opportunity to acquire these properties arose through the concerted efforts of the Nazi regime to divest Jewish owners of their economic assets, the so-called Aryanization campaign of the 1930s. Flick was deeply implicated in this campaign, although he remained wary throughout this period of the growing influence of the Nazi state in the economy. All the same, he worked assiduously to develop contacts and solidify ties among leading Nazi policymakers, most notably Hermann Göring and through membership in the so-called Circle of Friends of Heinrich Himmler, which offered Flick a degree of legitimacy in the Third Reich not available to most other businessmen. The experience he accrued in navigating the Nazi economic bureaucracy proved essential to his eventual acquisition of the Rombach steelworks in 1941.

Flick's career developed in tandem with Germany's turbulent history in the twentieth century.[1] Beginning with his appointment as director of a small regional steel concern, he cultivated a talent for accumulating wealth and influence through an intuitive grasp of the business possibilities inherent in any social or political situation. An observer of Germany's industrial scene in 1924 observed that Flick "was seized with the spirit of the times and felt himself likewise imbued with a mission. He sprang with both feet into the cauldron of the restructuring process, slipped beneath the surface a

couple of times and resurfaced as a new king of the heavy-industrial conglomerate. . . . Today Friedrich Flick—whose name is unknown to the public but who is renowned among fellow industrialists and bankers (who
abhor him, as he shuts them out) as one of the most powerful, successful,
and adroit businessmen."[2]

The speed with which Flick's economic stature grew distinguishes
his career in the annals of modern German business history. In 1926,
as Germany underwent a post-inflationary recovery, Flick's holdings
already ranked fifth among German producers of raw steel.[3] By 1937,
when he founded the Friedrich Flick Kommanditgesellschaft to exercise
central control over his diverse empire, output in his plants fell behind
only the levels of the enormous Vereinigte Stahlwerke (VSt) and Krupp.
By 1941, they had exceeded the latter, making his concern the largest privately controlled steel operation in Germany and second only to the collectively owned VSt in output. Throughout World War II, Flick moved
to exploit opportunities afforded by Germany's expansion in Europe to
enlarge his holdings and reinforce his position in German industry. His
concern was noteworthy for its efficiency as well as its scale: the principal parts of his sprawling operation achieved the most rapid consistent production increases of any German steel plants between 1929 and
1939, principally through the processing of scrap.[4] His steel operations
accounted for an impressive 52 percent of the total production increase
recorded in plants situated in the so-called Altreich, the core territories that comprised Germany before 1938.[5] Imprisonment from 1947 to
1951 for crimes against humanity failed to detract from his determination. Recognizing the potential for growth in the climate of the postwar
Bundesrepublik, the "collector of industrial participations" constructed
a postwar empire even more impressive than the one over which he had
presided in the Nazi era.[6]

His origins betray little of the potential his later success revealed.
Friedrich Flick was born on 10 July 1883 in Ernsdorf, Westphalia, the son
of a farmer with connections to the iron-ore mining industry in that area.
Flick recalled on the occasion of his sixtieth birthday that a career in the
iron industry had appealed to him from a very young age, perhaps by virtue
of how open possibilities for success seemed for a youth whose ambitions

exceeded the status of his birth. At twenty-one he performed military service, obligatory in the Kaiserreich, and thereafter attended a trade school in Cologne, where he graduated in 1907. Flick's first job after his schooling was that of Prokurist, a corporate official with power of attorney, with the Bremerhütte ore-processing plant in Wiedenau. He remained there for five years, departing in May 1913 to take up a position on the Vorstand, or governing board, of Menden & Schwerte, a steel enterprise in his home region of Siegerland. His prospects brightened on 1 April 1915 with appointment to a seat on the governing board of Charlottenhütte AG, an old steel firm founded in 1864. Flick later considered the position important for his subsequent efforts to erect a fully integrated steel concern. The economic circumstances of World War I provided a propitious backdrop to his efforts: by 1918 Flick had nearly doubled the value of his original holdings from RM 5 to 9.5 million through an aggressive series of acquisitions.[7] The latter included, among others, the immense Siegener Eisenbahnbedarf AG, a major producer of railroad equipment.

With the onset of the Weimar era, Flick began to cast about for growth prospects beyond the Siegerland.[8] He met with little initial success. His early impulse was to expand into the heavily developed Ruhr region, the country's industrial heartland, but his efforts to acquire an iron foundry as a toehold for further expansion were rebuffed by the cabal of industrialists who dominated the area. Instead he looked to opportunities in the eastern region of Upper Silesia, the boundaries of which were in dispute among the diplomats at Versailles. There Flick put together the components of a regionally based steel concern, acquiring in the short span of three years an iron foundry, mining operation, and steel processing plant. In 1920 he took over the Bismarckhütte, in 1921 the Kattowitzer Aktiengesellschaft für Bergbau und Hüttenbetrieb, and finally the Oberschlesische Eisenindustrie-Aktiengesellschaft and its assorted subcomponents, becoming through these acquisitions an "extraordinarily large force" in Silesia.[9]

By the early years of the Weimar Republic, then, Flick had already made a mark on German heavy industry. The established barons in the Ruhr took heed of his growing significance and offered him in 1923 a stake in an important Ruhr conglomerate called the Rhein-Elbe-Union. Through it, Flick's role in the formation of the Vereinigte Stahlwerke (VSt), "the largest private undertaking in this country,"[10] enhanced his standing in the German industrial community and led to his first significant exposure to the rough-and-tumble of Weimar politics. The VSt was a trust established by leading members of the steel industry in 1926 to regulate the production, distribution, and pricing of steel and steel products in the German market.[11] Two industrial magnates, Albert Vögler and Fritz Thyssen—the former of whom was quite friendly with Flick—spearheaded the drive to consolidate four large concerns into a single entity with a value of RM 800 million. Flick assumed a sizable stake as a result of his holdings in Gelsenkirchener Bergwerke, one of the largest parts of the Rhein-Elbe-Union, itself the largest single shareholder in the VSt. Apparently, Flick planned to purchase a majority stake in Gelsenberg, which through the Rhein-Elbe-Union would afford him majority control of the entire trust. With these transactions Flick had amassed a vast personal fortune and attained what he later described as his "highest industrial position" in terms of his net influence over the German steel community.[12]

The imperfect grasp of the trust on the German market for steel products quickly gave rise to problems that soured Flick on the new entity. Some steel producers declined to invest in it, while several had refused to cede control of their operations to the collective management structure. The collapse of American capital markets in 1929 dealt the VSt a heavy blow, since it had chosen to finance a substantial portion of its rationalization program with American money in the boom years of the mid-1920s. With the precarious financial basis of the trust exposed, the market worth of Flick's holdings declined to only 22 percent of their previous value and by 1932 his position threatened to unravel entirely.

Flick was not the sort of industrialist to be undone by an accident of fate. Glimpsing a chance to foist his burdens onto the German taxpayer, he embarked on a campaign to transfer ownership of his Gelsenberg shares to the German state.[13] In a series of dealings that led to his first significant contacts with the Nazi Party, Flick negotiated an agreement whereby the Reich government assumed his shares in the VSt for some 92 percent of their value, an astoundingly generous amount entirely disproportionate with the Reich government's obligations to maintain stability in the productive sector of the economy. Flick used the proceeds from the transaction to buy out his stake in the trust and reconsolidate his property under his direct control. The transaction need not have implied anything about his political affiliations had not two mainstream German newspapers, the *Frankfurter Zeitung* and *Kölnische Zeitung*, revealed the deal to the public on 19 June 1932, provoking a torrent of criticism from the political parties of the Reichstag and the rest of the German press. This unwelcome public attention, abhorrent to a man almost obsessively concerned with safeguarding his privacy, accounted for his early contact with the Nazi Party, according to Flick's postwar testimony.[14] The terms of the deal also reverberated throughout the heavy industrial community, bringing forth stinging criticism from the chieftains of the Ruhr and dividing the members of industry's highest informal body, the Ruhrlade. It further led to a rebuke from Chancellor Franz von Papen, who criticized government assistance for unsteady enterprises and vowed to privatize firms already under government control.

The German government declined to launch an official investigation into the terms of the transaction, but the deal did not escape political scrutiny altogether. A major Nazi economics publication, *Deutsche Volkswirtschaft*, excoriated Flick in August 1932 for crimes against the German people and argued for the nationalization of his property, indeed of all large conglomerates, in the event of a Nazi seizure of power. This denunciation notwithstanding, Hermann Göring, in his capacity as a Reichstag deputy of the Nazi Party, met with Flick to examine the details of the transaction and declared upon review that fault for the deal lay not with Flick but with the cabinet of Chancellor Heinrich Brüning, which had approved the deal officially on 21 June 1932. However, the results of Göring's review did not persuade Flick to become a staunch supporter of the National Socialists, at least not at that juncture. With a prudent businessman's desire to spread his risk, Flick arranged a series of financial contributions to political parties across the spectrum, ranging from the Social Democratic Party to the Nazi Party, with particular emphasis on the bourgeois parties of the right. As one historian put it, "Flick gave to the Nazis only a relatively small portion of the large sums he distributed across the political spectrum for political purposes in 1932. And what he did contribute to them he gave not because he wanted them to get power but because he wanted to insure himself and his shaky business venture against that eventuality."[15]

Despite Flick's coolness toward the Nazis in the early 1930s, pro-business elements within the party began to extend feelers in his direction. That a desire to lure Flick motivated Göring's favorable review of the Gelsenberg transaction cannot be ascertained, but it was at the height of the public outcry over it that Wilhelm Keppler, Hitler's unofficial adviser on economic issues, invited Flick to join a small circle of business luminaries and party officials to advise the Nazi Party on economic issues. Flick, hesitant to involve himself in a forum for policy, suggested his chief deputy, Otto Steinbrinck, in his stead.[16] This would prove a fateful step. Membership in the Keppler Circle provided an avenue into Nazi circles, introduction to personalities involved in later Aryanization campaigns and the rearmament drive, and a certain degree of legitimacy within the Nazi economic system.

Involvement with Keppler also marked the formal introduction of Steinbrinck into Nazi circles of some significance. Steinbrinck had been among Germany's most successful submarine commanders during World War I, become active in Flick's organization in 1925, and by the early 1930s assumed responsibility for the day-to-day conduct of Flick's holdings. Early contact with elements of the Nazi Party presaged Steinbrinck's role in the late 1930s as a conduit for communications between the Flick concern and the Nazi government. Much more opportunistic than his boss, Steinbrinck became a member of the Nazi Party in May 1933, joined the SS shortly thereafter, and was promoted by 1939 to the lofty rank of Brigadeführer on the staff of the Reichsführer SS, Heinrich Himmler. Until his departure from the Flick concern in late 1939, Steinbrinck's numerous connections to senior members of the armed forces, government bureaucracies, and Nazi Party organization factored into the Flick concern's success in navigating the economic terrain of the 1930s. Flick himself did not join the Keppler Circle until 1936 (by then dominated by Heinrich Himmler and called the "Circle of Friends") and did not join the Nazi Party until 1937, by which point lack of membership would have arguably worked against his interests.[17] The function of the group centered less on discussion of economic policy than on serving as a channel for funds to the SS.

Flick's early contacts with the Nazi Party are a backdrop to the involvement of his conglomerate in the expropriation of Jewish industrial assets before World War II, a series of events that rank among the most complex confronting historians of the Third Reich. Flick acquired the Hochofenwerk Lübeck and substantial portions of the Julius and Ignaz Petschek groups after a series of protracted negotiations involving his concern, the Jewish owners, and various organs of the Nazi Party and state. That Flick's participation was significant in these instances is not in dispute; prior historical research has established the extent and nature of his involvement with an eye to its implications for racial policy in the Third Reich.[18] The cases depicted here shed light on the motives informing Flick's decisions as well as on the character of his relations with the Nazi regime and the economic bureaucracy. By 1940, when Flick undertook to acquire industrial assets under German control in the occupied West, he had already implicated himself in the economic program of the Nazi regime in Germany. The same opportunism that motivated him to exploit the disenfranchisement of the Jews informed his pursuit of assets in those western territories that fell under German control in 1940.

The chief beneficiaries of the Aryanization campaigns were not only the Nazi state, which furthered its ideological agenda, or party cronies, who expected to profit from the spoils, but the businesses and industrialists who engaged in sometimes-bitter rivalries to plunder their Jewish competition. But the overall picture is more complex than the foregoing point suggests. In addition to producers, the largest German banks also played a prominent, but by no means unambiguous, role in the process. Harold James has shown how the Deutsche Bank alternatively collected commissions for coordinating the transfer of property while in some instances cautiously helping the dispossessed Jewish owners to retain at least a portion of their wealth.[19] Even within the industrial community, the point in time at which specific Aryanizations occurred conditioned responses to them. By and large, as Peter Hayes has pointed out, most German firms initially assumed an ambivalent stance toward the Aryanization drive, demonstrating "little rush and some reluctance" before 1938.[20] Flick's experiences in those cases in which he played a role support this insight.

The first campaign in which Flick had a hand, if an indecisive one, was the Aryanization of the Waffenfabrik Simson in the city of Suhl, Thuringia. Better known then as now as a manufacturer of motorbikes, Simson was throughout the Weimar period the only German firm permitted under the terms of the Versailles Treaty to manufacture military small arms. The economic prospects of the firm in 1934 were bright: it had an annual turnover of some RM 18 million along with a physical plant valued at RM 9 million, a virtually captive market for its military products, and an established position in what promised to become a lively sector of the economy. The firm's only vulnerability was that its founder and director, Arthur Simson, was Jewish. Simson also had the misfortune of being located in the Gau led by Fritz Sauckel, who was among the most rabidly anti-Semitic of the Gauleiters. Following a withering propaganda campaign to provoke unrest among the firm's labor force, the criminal police launched an investigation into the firm's having allegedly garnered profits in excess of those stipulated in his contracts with official agencies. Under pressure, Simson agreed in early February 1934 to a trusteeship in which he retained formal ownership and capital shares, but surrendered practical control over the firm's operations. Unsatisfied with this partial outcome and seeking to ensure a "smooth cooperation" between itself and the firm, the Army Ordnance Office invited Flick in October 1934 to purchase the entire works.[21] Flick agreed to consider the invitation on the basis of both national strategic priorities and purely economic considerations.[22] However, given his desire to secure a reliable supply of pig iron before building more manufacturing capacity, his interest in acquiring Simson/Suhl appears to have waned.[23]

With no suitable buyer in sight, the Nazi regime pleaded with the Flick concern in late May 1935 to enter into a fresh round of negotiations with the increasingly harried Arthur Simson. Speaking with the Army Ordnance Office, Steinbrinck upheld a distinction between the legitimate legal interests and activities of private businessmen and those of the Nazi regime.[24] The state would have to Aryanize the company independent of any initiative from Flick. Should the Nazi regime choose to confiscate Simson/Suhl and later sell it off, he went on to say, then Flick was receptive to purchase under different terms. Flick refused even at that juncture to abandon his reservations over the economic viability of the enterprise and its congruence with his concern's long-term interests.[25]

The regime took over Simson/Suhl in December 1935 on the basis of an order from Hitler himself. The firm was placed in trusteeship in 1936 and transformed into a "model" Nazi corporation, with living quarters and retirement facilities for the plant's labor force.[26] Sauckel named the new venture "The Wilhelm Gustloff Foundation" after a Swiss who had allegedly died at the hands of "international high finance."[27] In his subsequent dealings with the Nazi regime, Flick would not forget the outcome of the Simson/Suhl debacle and the decisive role played in it by the Nazi Party. Flick had shown himself willing, despite the clearly anti-Semitic origins of the attack on Simson, to contemplate the acquisition of the firm when solicited by certain agencies of the regime.[28] But the absence of any apparent ideological component to his decision accentuates Flick's amorality in business affairs.

Flick's refusal to acquire Simson/Suhl on behalf of the regime came at a critical juncture in industry-state relations in the Third Reich. Industrialists could not have doubted by then that the Nazi government, already two years in office, would oversee large increases in construction and armaments spending, which promised great benefits and a turn from the stagnation that had plagued the German economy for half a decade. Indeed, a recent study has revealed that the immediate upswing in armaments spending under the Nazis allowed heavy industrial firms to exploit the substantial idle or underutilized productive capacity built up during the investment boom of the late-1920s, garnering large profits and high returns on capital.[29] The heavy industrial sector of the economy expanded by nearly 200 percent between 1932 and 1938, whereas consumer industries grew by only 38 percent.[30] To realize the regime's priorities in critical industrial sectors, "obstacles and obstructions" such as labor unions, factory councils, and working-class organizations devoted to labor emancipation were suppressed or incorporated into the Nazi social system through a ruthless *Gleichschaltung*, allowing the industrialist to reassert his traditional authority as Herr im Haus.[31]

However, industrialists were hard-pressed to ignore the opposite side of the ledger. By the mid-1930s it was also apparent that the Third Reich was hardly a businessman's regime, serving to reinforce an authoritarian brand of capitalism. The extent to which the Nazi regime determined industry-state relations will always remain a contentious issue, but historians have little doubt that the establishment of the Reichswerke Hermann Göring in

1937 was a major watershed. From that point on, the export-oriented, conservative influence of Hjalmar Schacht, a conservative who served as economics minister after 1934, declined irrevocably, while Hermann Göring, as head of the Four-Year Plan organization, spearheaded the rise of a Nazi technocratic elite devoted to bringing the authoritarian power of the regime to bear on the economy in a push for self-sufficiency.[32] Under such circumstances, as David Schoenbaum observed, the status of business in the Third Reich became "at best the product of a social contract between unequal partners, in which submission was the condition for success."[33]

Deference to the Nazi state's priorities in no way precluded the opportunity to prosper. Peter Hayes has shown that IG Farben, after an initial period of ambivalence, was drawn to the economic ambitions of the regime out of a perceived congruity of interests. The placement of technical personnel and managers from the firm in the offices of the new Four-Year Plan organization expedited its "Nazification," although dissent within the firm persisted.[34] The example of IG Farben notwithstanding, the fulfillment of the Nazi regime's economic goals benefited from the shifting landscape of German industrial life, which produced in turn a new business ethos and set of political orientations. The push for economic self-sufficiency afforded prominence to professional technocrats, scientists, and engineers, "many of whom were attracted to Nazism not because of its radicalism, but because it offered opportunities through massive state projects to master technical problems without financial constraint."[35] These new circumstances placed the leaders of traditional industries in a bind. On the one hand, they could not afford to ignore the opportunities provided by rearmament, state-sponsored building projects, or Aryanization for fear of abandoning the field to competitors. At the same time, increased cooperation with the regime deepened their dependency upon it, both in the material form of actual contracts and in the ethical form of underpinning Nazi rule as "silent partners."[36]

With the advent of the Four-Year Plan and a stepped-up pace of rearmament in 1936, the economic circumstances under which the steel industry particularly had operated before then altered dramatically.[37] Paul Pleiger, later an official in Göring's economic organization, had investigated the possibility of using poor-quality native ores in the Salzgitter region even before the advent of the Four-Year Plan. He and Keppler had approached dubious Ruhr industrialists, including Steinbrinck, as early as February 1935 to lobby them for the initial investment required.[38] Few industrialists could have imagined that even a government as unorthodox in its thinking as the Nazi regime would go through with a plan so contrary, in their view, to sound economic sense. The founding of the Reichswerke on 23 July 1937, therefore, intensified domestic competition for the nation's stretched coal reserves and left the steel barons shaken. As Flick put it after the war, "it was quite a surprise for us so far as we had not thought that the whole problem would be solved with such an intensity and with such a power used by the State."[39] As German coal and steel firms had only recently begun to recover from the Depression and remained reluctant to expand capacity, conflicts between them and the regime's new enterprise were unavoidable.

It remains arguable whether a concerted opposition from Germany's steel barons stood any chance of destroying the Reichswerke program before it became a serious threat, or whether an earlier willingness to exploit domestic ore deposits would have headed off its foundation. Regardless, leading industrialists opted for a path of opposition. Ernst Poensgen and Albert Vögler of the VSt headed a campaign against the Reichswerke that produced the so-called Düsseldorf memorandum, formulated in a series of meetings between Germany's leading industrialists (and monitored secretly by Göring, who had wiretapped their phones).[40] The memorandum set forth their objections in a manner that left no doubt as to their antipathy to the intentions of the regime.[41] At this point, Flick distinguished himself from the other major figures in preferring a course of accommodation to one of opposition. At a meeting on 20 August 1937, he suggested that the large coal and steel firms volunteer to establish a collective private operation devoted to exploiting low-grade domestic ores in lieu of a state-sponsored enterprise.[42] His position was essentially pragmatic: in failing to advance an alternative program that addressed the regime's strategic intentions, Flick believed that industry would unnecessarily push itself into an unfavorable opposition to the Nazi regime. Although a handful of industrialists supported Flick's motion, the majority favored a principled stand. In the end, it came to nothing. Few possessed the moral courage to resist official pressure: several, including Flick, received a warning from

Göring likening opposition to the Reichswerke to sabotage and refused to sign the memorandum.[43] The prospects for a united front against the Reichswerke dissolved.

During the deliberations, Flick began exploring ways to safeguard his position rather than become ensnared in a dispute over the autonomy of private industry and the market for steel. A firm in his concern, Maxhütte, had already begun exploiting low-grade domestic ores in the Dogger region. Anticipating that the Reichswerke would require him to cede some of Maxhütte's ore mines, Flick resolved to give up those holdings preemptively, "in opposition to other leaders of the German iron and steel industry," as Göring put it.[44] Flick's desire to accommodate the regime did not go unnoticed. In a personal note to Flick, Göring expressed his pleasure at ongoing negotiations between the Reichswerke and Flick's firm, which suggests that more concessions may have been in store. Even as this transpired, Flick continued to play a role in the fruitless inter-industry discussions on a common policy against the Reichswerke. One might account for the contradiction as a cynical attempt to safeguard his settlement with the regime by sabotaging effective opposition to the Reichswerke. However, the opportunism conspicuous in Flick's decision-making in other cases suggests rather that he had not yet settled unreservedly on the path of accommodation and desired to keep his options open.[45] In the end, the rest of the industrial community did not hold his opportunism against him. Seven of the largest steel firms empowered Flick, along with Peter Klöckner, in October 1937 to negotiate a surrender to the Reichswerke in which the steel industry declared itself ready to aid in the development of the new effort and invest a hefty sum in its operations.[46]

The Reichswerke crisis broke the back of overt industrial opposition to Nazi policy in the iron and steel sector of the economy. In presenting big businessmen with the threat of nationalization should they fail to cooperate, the regime forced them to confront the stark reality of its intentions. The steel industrialists never again attempted to mount a joint opposition to the Nazi regime's economic programs. Flick's own reconciliation with the Reichswerke foreshadowed this more general retreat on the part of industrialists to their parochial interests and an abandonment of efforts to defend the concept of private industry as such. In 1937, this fragmentation also reflected the Flick concern's peculiar outsider status among the traditional leading ranks of Germany's coal and steel industry, particularly those of the Ruhr. Private concerns like that of Flick found a flexible approach to the regime expedient by virtue of their aggravated vulnerability to market forces within a structurally rigid industry.[47] By virtue of their tenuous position, "newly ascendant enterprises in key industries . . . were opting to hitch their individual wagons to the star of Nazi policy far more firmly than their elders had been inclined to do."[48] Hereafter, having seen the determination of the regime to rid the economy of Jewish influence and override industrial opposition to its measures, Flick choose to profit where he may.

Flick's opportunism found its best expression in the accelerating Aryanization campaign of the late 1930s. As it happened, the Flick concern had a preexisting relationship with one of the regime's first significant targets in the steel sector. The Hochofenwerk Lübeck was the largest of that city, drawing on high-quality Scandinavian ore to produce pig iron, cement, and copper as well as gas and electricity.[49] Four firms in "non-Aryan" hands controlled RM 14.3 million of its RM 16 million net worth. The ownership of one of the firms, however, was extremely heterogeneous and included not only Jews but a large number of foreign investors, who controlled approximately 68 percent of its stock. This foreign proprietorship complicated matters enormously in the mid-1930s. As a rule, the Nazi regime trod carefully with firms that had a high proportion of foreign ownership, fearing the international repercussions stemming from seizure or excessive harassment.

In mid-January 1935, a former member of Hochofenwerk Lübeck's Vorstand approached Flick regarding the possible purchase of a majority of Lübeck's shares.[50] As the offer addressed Flick's desire to secure a supply of pig iron, he had Steinbrinck draw up a plan whereby his Mittelstahl would acquire a majority stake. In the meantime, the Army Ordnance Office approached Flick in the interest of having the firm taken over by a non-Jewish owner.[51] When it became clear with the negotiations that a controlling interest could not be had, however, Flick abruptly opted out.[52]

Eager to try other avenues, Flick focused his attention on one of the two smaller firms with sizable holdings in Lübeck. By acquiring 51 percent of the stock in the smaller firm, Flick could gain direct control over its slice of the Lübeck works.[53] At a meeting of 1 December 1937, pressure from the Nazi regime divided the unified front thrown up by three of the holding company's foreign shareholders.[54] Flick took control of the stock and purged the supervisory and governing boards of the firm, leaving him free to pursue the remainder of the shares.[55]

Negotiations with the remaining Jewish owners, who had founded the Lübeck works and retained control of 60 percent of its shares, foundered initially on the price and size of the purchase. Flick drove a hard bargain, insisting that they offer up their entire holdings, instead of the minimum amount required to secure majority control in the Lübeck works.[56] Perhaps recognizing the ultimate futility of their position, the owners offered to settle with Flick provided that he secure a *Beruhigungserklärung*, or reassurance decree, guaranteeing their exemption from further persecution.[57] Flick found these terms acceptable. He had no difficulty obtaining the reassurance decree they sought and Mittelstahl duly acquired a controlling interest in Lübeck on 10 January 1938.[58]

Flick's interest in the Lübeck works was rooted in business calculations and he outwardly conducted negotiations with the shareholders in good faith. None of his opponents were arrested or placed in "protective custody." In legalistic terms, the process whereby the Lübeck works were brought into Flick's hands appeared "voluntary" and reflected legitimate business activity. However, one could not overlook the fact that he required the regime's reassurance decree to persuade the final group of shareholders to relinquish their stake. Clearly, fear of persecution was a major factor in their calculations.

Even as the acquisition of Hochofenwerk Lübeck proceeded apace in November 1937, Flick was positioning his concern to participate in an effort of much greater scope: the Aryanization of the vast Petschek mining concern. Flick sought to acquire the smaller of the two (the Anhaltische Kohlenwerke AG and Werschenweissenfelser AG—AKW-WW) as a reliable source of lignite for his expanding Mitteldeutsche Stahlwerke. His own reserves were not projected to last beyond another two and a half decades.[59] Through contacts in the former Keppler Circle, Flick maneuvered to place himself at the forefront of the parties vying for the spoils.

The question of state interference rapidly came to the fore. At a meeting with Steinbrinck in early November, Keppler expressed a desire to coordinate a joint effort among the interested parties to drive down the price demanded by the Petscheks.[60] He further suggested appointing a state official to lead the negotiations in lieu of representatives from the competing firms. The possibility of direct state intervention troubled Flick, for whom the increasingly intense competition for lignite in central Germany had become a nagging concern.[61] Propitiously enough for Flick, however, considerable apprehension persisted among Nazi officials over the foreign repercussions of direct state action. Steinbrinck managed in late November to persuade the regime to uphold a facade of "voluntary" or "legal" expropriation involving a private buyer for the sake of not exposing German firms operating abroad to retaliation.[62] Owing to the size of the AKW-WW's reserves, Hermann Göring had developed an acute interest in the outcome and reserved for himself the right to determine the allocation of the assets.[63] Accordingly, Flick encouraged closer relations with state officials throughout late 1937 in the hope of securing for his firm as large a proportion of the Petschek mines as possible.[64]

The tendency toward greater state involvement, so worrisome to Flick and Steinbrinck, intensified in 1938. On 4 January, Hermann Göring decided that "the whole question [of the Petscheks] should be centralized and dealt with by him personally . . . thus excluding the possibility of official action," a spurious distinction at best.[65] However, in a remarkable move that underscored Flick's increasing closeness to the Nazi regime, Göring personally granted him on 21 January 1938 exclusive authority to conduct negotiations with the Petschek groups.[66] Through this special dispensation, which eliminated the possibility of competitive bidding, the price of a settlement would presumably decline. Although Göring retained the right to determine the final distribution of the holdings, Flick probably expected to receive a favorable allotment by virtue of his central role.

Negotiations carried out with the American representative of the Petscheks between 26 and 28 January 1938 revealed the increasingly blurry relationship between private industry and the regime's power in Flick's thinking.[67] Difficulties arose immediately and the talks remained deadlocked until the fourth day, when Flick alluded to the possibility of direct action by the regime should they fail to resolve the issue privately. As such an outcome had previously been undesirable to Flick, one must note the significance of his shift in tactics.[68]

Flick's threat failed to have the desired effect and the parties remained at an impasse for more than a month. Steinbrinck reported in mid-February that the Petscheks had "protected themselves well" and speculated that they awaited a sign of more decisive action by the Nazi regime.[69] In the event, it was Germany's takeover of Austria in early March and its souring relations with Czechoslovakia that finally induced the Petscheks to crack.[70] A settlement was authorized by Hermann Göring and the Economics Ministry on 25 May 1938, clearing the way for a consortium headed by Flick to distribute the different parts of the property among Mittelstahl and two outside firms.[71]

Flick's proceedings with the Julius Petschek group had the additional purpose of making more pliable the larger of the two Petschek groups, the Ignaz Petschek concern.[72] Early on it became clear that the regime would play a more prominent role in this case than in earlier ones.[73] The Ignaz Petschek group had coal mining operations throughout central Germany, Czechoslovakia, and Austria. Collectively, these companies controlled somewhat less than one-third of all lignite in Germany and exercised formidable power within the East Elbian Coal Syndicate. Moreover, the owners were well aware of their importance and determined not to give up their shares easily.[74]

A lawyer for the Flick concern came forward with a solution. He suggested formulating a series of decrees appointing a trustee to execute the requirements of the Four-Year Plan in plants owned or controlled by Jews. Shareholders, whose privileges would be ignored, would forfeit rights to their shares, and foreign groups would be required to register their holdings.[75] However, the results of a meeting among several agencies of the Nazi government, of which Steinbrinck learned through an official source, underlined the reluctance of the regime to appoint a commissioner, expropriate the property outright, or undertake any violent or coercive measures.[76]

Perhaps mindful of the worsening situation for Jews in Germany, the Petscheks resolved to enter negotiations and indicated a preference for a single negotiator with full powers. The Nazi regime assured Flick that he would be invited to conduct the negotiations as soon as the Petscheks consented to a format.[77] Before details were resolved, the Nazi regime decided to dispense with further legal niceties and impose an independent solution. On the authority of the Four-Year Plan, a general decree of 3 December 1938 provided for a trustee to superintend those enterprises defined as Jewish by earlier decree.[78] As Flick retained sole formal authority to negotiate with the Petscheks by virtue of his January 1938 mandate from Göring, Steinbrinck seized the opportunity to lobby the Economics Ministry that Flick was the most logical choice for administering the assets, from the perspective of both his industrial competence as well as his wide experience in mergers and negotiations.[79]

The state rebuffed Flick's offer. On 19 January 1939, the Economics Ministry designated a state official to be temporary trustee for the management of the Petschek enterprises. The appointment signaled the end of efforts to pursue the expropriation of Jewish industrial assets in a quasi-legal manner and underscored the purely instrumental manner in which the Nazis had sought to use Flick's willingness to accommodate its wishes. Because the regime threatened to nullify earlier guarantees that the final distribution of assets would consider Flick's interests, the regime's rejection of private negotiations threw into doubt the motives behind his collaboration.

Flick immediately launched a campaign to win some part of the spoils for himself through negotiations with the Economics Ministry, the Four-Year Plan organization, and the Reichswerke. In his approach he sought to exploit the Reichswerke's need for a supply of hard-coal, with which the latter hoped to bypass the collective pricing of the Ruhr coal syndicates.[80] Flick had a controlling interest in two-hard coal operations and was willing to exchange parts of them for a reliable central German supply of lignite.[81] Accordingly, he reached an agreement on 9 December 1939 that provided for an exchange of reserves from Flick's Harpen mines for a sizable collection of lignite mines.[82] The arrangement was not a certain triumph for Flick: in the end he surrendered more of his valuable hard-coal reserves and received less lignite than he had hoped.[83] In addition, the preamble and postscript to the contract, assigning responsibility for the transaction to the regime and the national economic interest, were stricken from the final agreement, making it clear that his desire to profit from the spoils of racial policy was perhaps only marginally less pronounced than that of the Nazi regime.

Flick's machinations make clear that straightforward business considerations defined his interactions with the Nazi regime throughout the early years of its rule, especially his participation in the Aryanization campaign of the late 1930s. The evidence does not indicate identification with the racial agenda or ideological program of the Nazi regime. Especially after the founding of the Reichswerke in 1936, Flick resolved largely to conform rather than risk martyrdom in his dealings with the regime. He revealed himself as adept at evoking the potential of state intervention to justify his early acquisitions of the Lübeck works and the Julius Petschek properties, and proved willing to solicit Hermann Göring's support in restraining other private firms from competing for the same assets. Finally, he cited Göring's mandate of January 1938 on numerous occasions as a means of legitimating his concern's inclusion in the distribution of the Ignaz group's lignite holdings. It was an indifference bred of opportunism that drove Flick to take actions that served as much as anything else to imperil the integrity of private enterprise in Germany over the long term.

Chapter 3

The German Steel Industry before the Assimilation of Lorraine and Plans for Expropriation

As has been seen, territorial conquest and economic expansion, justified through a matrix of ruthless ideological and racial beliefs, were twin pillars of the Nazi program in Europe. Economic aggrandizement was thought to be fundamental to the success of the Nazi racial mission, even if the precise contours and implications of the effort were never elaborated fully before 1938. In the belief that a broad program of territorial and economic expansion was necessary to the future prospects of the German people, the Nazi movement built on a long tradition of thinking that extended back into the nineteenth century. Only the nakedly racist and exterminatory underpinnings of Nazism's imperial mission were novel, even if its superficial implications on a practical economic level resembled notions elaborated before and during World War I.[1]

The Nazi regime could count on the broad support of the German industrial community in fulfilling these ambitions. In a manner reminiscent of the quasi-Darwinist, zero-sum economic logic of Nazism, leading industrialists had for decades before World War II argued privately and publicly that a wider basis of resources and productive potential were necessary for Germany to survive in competition with the other nations of Europe. As Nazi aggression began in earnest in 1938, the industrial community found itself reckoning with both the remarkable opportunities for expansion and the regime's own intentions and practical efforts toward dominating the economic landscape of Europe. Particularly in Central and Western Europe, highly developed foreign industrial plants were seen as ripe targets for expropriation and incorporation into the German war effort. The critical question turned on the roles of the key agents involved and the specific form the resulting arrangements would assume.

Narrowly understood, the conquest of Lorraine in 1940 allowed the Nazi regime to address what was thought to be the most alarming vulnerability of the German war economy before the outbreak of war in 1939, namely the lack of a secure domestic ore base for the steel industry. Based on a retrospective view of the war effort, planners may have been overly pessimistic in assuming that Germany would be without deep reserves of such a critical resource. However, contemporary indications seemed to point in the direction of troubling inadequacies in steel production, a problem exacerbated by the general confusion that prevailed in economic planning and policy generally. By the time Lorraine became a part of the German sphere of influence, there existed broad support in industrial circles for a thoroughgoing expropriation of the steel firms there.

No economic sector was as fundamental to the ability of Germany to wage a major war as that of iron and steel, and here the outlook in Germany seemed grim in the late 1930s. Concerns about the inadequate ore and processing base of the steel industry reflected long-standing perceptions of German vulnerability to a protracted war effort based on industrial output. As early as 1907 a professor at the Berlin Academy of Mining, Hermann Wedding, wrote that in war, "three factors play a leading role in every country—men, foodstuffs, and the raw materials of iron manufacturing. It is worthwhile to consider during peace the extent to which these three factors are available, so as to avoid disappointments in the event of war." A prudent German government, he continued, would take care to ensure that "iron ore, as the raw material of that metal most crucial to the power and well-being of a nation, can be secured within the country itself."[2] By the terms of the Treaty of Versailles in 1919, Germany ceded its richest domestic sources of high-grade ore to France. The great steelworks of Lorraine had provided the German economy with some 20 percent of its pig iron, 12 percent of its basic steel, and nearly 80 percent of its ore.[3] As a result, the interwar German steel industry came to rely heavily upon imported ore, with Sweden, France, and Spain accounting for nearly 77.6 percent of German inputs in 1935.[4]

With the disastrous effects of the blockade in World War I in mind, the Nazi regime wrestled with various measures throughout the 1930s to lessen dependence on foreign sources of iron ore.[5] Its efforts culminated in the

Four-Year Plan of 1936, launched with a twofold purpose: in the near term, to safeguard the German economy against international crises and fluctuations in demand for German exports, and in the longer term, to lay the economic foundations of a future war effort against a blockade, "without regard for the costs," as Hitler put it. The crowning achievement of the program was the massive state-sponsored Reichswerke, which sought through the intensified mining of domestic ores "to raise Germany's iron production to the very utmost."[6] The implications of the effort—lower quality and more expensive pig iron for the steel industry, stunted profitability, and the metallurgical uncertainty of the necessary processes—were simply dismissed or ignored by supporters of the project. The Reichswerke met with only limited success; by 1939 some 32 percent of German ore derived from domestic sources, a figure that owed much to the assimilation of Austria and Czechoslovakia in 1938–39.[7] But the program had other merits as well. Ease of extraction and access to transportation networks were important priorities for an ore supply under wartime conditions, and ore from central Germany retained those advantages over imported varieties until the assimilation of the great ore fields of Lorraine and Luxemburg in 1940.

The benefits of convenience extended only so far, however. The issue of economic optimization was bound to make a lasting solution to Germany's rearmament problems highly improbable. German ore had a much lower iron content (approximately 30 percent) relative to that from Sweden (approximately 60 percent). Although transportation costs increased the price of Swedish ore, that cost was partially offset by the much greater volume of pig iron that could be smelted from it. Moreover, per ton of pig iron output, higher-grade ores required a smaller workforce and less coking coal, and made correspondingly lower demands on blast-furnace capacity.[8] These shortcomings were not insignificant and were made worse by the circumstances of German rearmament. Scarce mining labor and the inefficiencies of the transportation system in Germany combined to create a continuous shortfall in coking coal, making high-grade ore a preferable alternative to domestic varieties. This preference is reflected in usage figures: if measured by the content of the ore used, German dependence on foreign sources in 1938 still hovered around 70 percent.[9] Finally, scrap constituted a major input in steel production along with pig iron. A sizable proportion of scrap used in the German steel industry came from countries that would clearly become enemies of Germany in the event of war, rendering potential wartime levels of steel production uncertain and necessitating expensive adjustments of plant to new inputs.[10] In response to these facts, Reichsbank chief and former economics minister Hjalmar Schacht said in a speech in November 1938 that Germany was neither then autarkic nor ever likely to become so, a fact that, given his opposition to the Reichswerke from the outset, undoubtedly gratified him to point out.[11]

Despite the efforts of the regime, then, the German steel industry on the eve of the Western campaign seemed unlikely to wean itself from its dependence on foreign sources of ore. At one point, the German Economics Ministry official responsible for iron and steel production underscored in a conference with leading steel producers that a reliable and cost-effective supply of ore was the single most pressing issue in rearmament.[12] Among the major combatants of World War II, only Japan and Italy were even less self-supporting than Germany, a state of affairs that failed to impress the leader of the Axis alliance enough to make them reconsider their plans.

Historians have argued in one form or another that organizational malfeasance underlay what was seen as a marked shortage of steel, particularly in the distribution of it within and between integrated concerns.[13] But one should not overlook the lack of foreign exchange as a factor limiting expansion of German production and an easing of the production bottlenecks. The war economy in the late 1930s suffered acute shortages of steel for armaments manufacturing chiefly as a result of an inability to finance additional imports of Swedish ores, despite the fact that the steel industry was operating at 83 percent capacity.[14] Without hard currency to pay for the importation of additional ores, industry stood no chance of fulfilling the huge rearmament programs of the Wehrmacht. The German economy underwent a succession of crises throughout the 1930s defined by the increasing difficulty of balancing export production, which was necessary to secure foreign exchange, with rearmament production. Only a series of interventions by Schacht, then Reich Minister of Economics, and the curtailment of the most excessive military procurement programs averted collapse. By the late 1930s, foreign suppliers of crucial raw materials had become reluctant to accept German credit against deliveries and insisted on

hard currency.[15] By 1938 Germany had stockpiled reserves of iron ore sufficient to cover only three months of full production.[16] Of the approximately
10.5 million tons imported in 1938, only the ore from Sweden, Norway,
and neutral Western Europe, amounting to roughly 50 percent, could be
assured in the near term.[17] As the latter sources were strategically vulnerable, German planners could actually count only on the Swedish ore.[18]

The incorporation of Lorraine into a contiguous German economic
area, immune from foreign-exchange fluctuations, therefore held out the
prospect of some measure of relief for a steel industry severely over-
stretched and insecurely supplied on the eve of war. The German need for
more reliable and inexpensive sources of ore does not appear to have factored directly into strategic intentions to break out of the operational stale-
mate in the West in 1940, but some historians, notably Alan Milward, have
discerned a clear connection, pointing out that German dependence on
imported ore could prove troublesome for Nazi Germany: "The possibility
of an alternative source of supply made iron ore appear as the most valuable commodity which the French economy had to offer Germany."[19] This
fact was appreciated by Hitler himself. As Göring indicated in a conference
in January 1940, "[The Führer] had singled out the industrial areas of Donai
and Lens and those of Luxemburg. Longwy and Briey [the chief ore-min-
ing districts of eastern France] could, from the point of view of raw materials, replace the supplies from Sweden."[20] Given the economic vulnerabilities
of Germany's strategic situation, German planners realized that the steel
industry of Lorraine promised a crucial impetus to German armaments
production.[21] Some 15.5 million tons of ore was mined in Lorraine alone in
1938, an amount exceeding that extracted in Germany as a whole.
Acquisition of the industrial plants there would increase total German output of pig iron and basic, unfinished steel by 55 percent and 47 percent
respectively, a potential boon for war production.[22] The combined Austrian
and Czech mining and processing industries, incorporated over the pre-
ceding two years and taken over largely by the state-economic apparatus,
paled in comparison with the vast resources of eastern France. Few other
alternatives could secure what Otto Fitzner, chief of the metals section in
the Economics Ministry, characterized as the overarching economic ambition of the Nazi regime, namely "to bring about those conditions which

will secure the economic and military sovereignty of the German people for as long as possible."[23]

The German steel industry in the early years of the twentieth century cannot be understood apart from Lorraine.[24] After the German victory in the Franco-Prussian War of 1871, the Imperial regime annexed the region along with Alsace and governed it through a local proxy nominally appointed by the emperor. Little noteworthy economic activity took place in the first years of German rule, however. The expense involved in processing the relatively low-quality ores (30–35 percent iron content) located along the Moselle River undermined the economic rationale for exploiting them.[25] Full realization of Lorraine's potential for steel production came about only after the introduction of the Gilchrist-Thomas process in 1879, which made feasible the inexpensive manufacture of steel from phosphoric raw iron.

With that innovation, the floodgates of German investment opened in earnest, leading to the construction of numerous mine heads and steelworks stoked by coking coal from the Ruhr.[26] A major industry report from the spring of 1927 retrospectively characterized the development of the Thomas process as a "milestone in the history of the German iron industry" and the exploitation of Lorraine's ores as a "question of life" for Germany, and noted that the incorporation of Lorraine into the Reich resolved at a stroke Germany's "most urgent concerns."[27] Investments by German concerns had the effect of integrating Lorraine tightly into the fabric of German industrial development. On account of the low iron content of the ore there (called minette) and high cost of transporting it over the 350 km stretch between Lorraine and the Ruhr (the Mosel River was not easily navigable downriver from Metz), traffic between the two regions was largely one way. Smelting a ton of raw iron in the Ruhr required the shipment of three tons of minette from Lorraine, whereas plants in Lorraine could smelt the same amount of iron with only a single ton of coking coal from Ruhr collieries. The advantages in smelting the ore in Lorraine outweighed the costs of transporting coking coal from the Ruhr to such an extent that the price of pig iron in Lorraine normally undercut that within the Ruhr by several marks throughout the Imperial period, approaching at times the exceptionally low *Selbstkosten* (the internal cost to the plant of producing a given quantity of steel) of vertically integrated concerns there.[28] Along with Luxemburg (by this time a part of the German customs zone), Lorraine soon accounted for nearly three-quarters of Germany's usable iron ore and provided an important basis for Germany's production throughout World War I.[29] The immense importance of Lorraine's ore fields and steel plants for the war economy was the subject of a lengthy 1917 memorandum by the leading members of the German steel industry to Count von Hertling, the Imperial chancellor, and Field Marshall von Hindenburg. Discounting the reliability of ore supplies from Sweden and Spain, and the improbability of consistent support from Russia, the memorandum maintained that "[h]ad we lost Lorraine, even if the production of the other German mines had been increased, it would not have been possible to wage the present war on three fronts at once."[30]

Defeat in World War I brought German exploitation of the Lorraine minette fields to an end.[31] The steelworks of the Rhine-Westphalian region in particular forfeited nearly two-thirds of their domestic ore inputs. In addition to losing its unfettered control over the resources of Lorraine, German industry lost some of its most modern and valuable smelting operations and steel plants as well. The bitter aftertaste of this loss lingered among Germany industrialists and policymakers for two decades. A penetrating study from January 1940 on the lessons of the previous two decades for Germany's critical economic sectors underscored that the country's "battles in the world war were waged with iron produced above all in Lorraine."[32] The terms of the Versailles settlement in 1919 effectively ruptured the organic connections that had arisen between the Ruhr and Lorraine processing plants over the previous fifty years.[33] Broadly viewed over the longer term, while in 1913 Germany produced approximately 28.5 million tons of iron ore with 8.5 million tons of iron content, output by 1932 had sunk to 4 million tons of ore with an iron content of about 1.3 million tons.[34]

The process whereby the French government expropriated the steelworks of Lorraine after World War I embittered the German industrial community nearly as much as the loss of the works themselves. The war had been ruinous for the French steel industry, with ore processing and raw iron production falling continually between 1914 and 1918 to catastrophically low levels. The French government, moreover, had financed the war effort by accumulating massive amounts of debt, chiefly from the United States, and was compelled in the immediate postwar period to devise ways of reviving industrial production to service that debt and bring about a more general recovery. The broad belt of industry stretching across Lorraine thus held out as much economic promise for the French as it had for the Germans. For the most part, the French authorities summarily expelled the German founders of the steel firms in Lorraine and only later offered restitution that amounted to a small fraction of the value of the assets forfeited.[35] The collective memory of the expropriation process after World War I undoubtedly played a part in the reflexive readiness of many German industrialists to see the seizure of the resources and plants of Lorraine as justified in 1940.

Like many other German social groups in the Weimar era, German iron and steel industrialists devoted a great deal of publicity to what they held to be the inequitable character of the Versailles settlement and devised initiatives to redress it. In December 1919, a consortium of sixteen German iron and steel firms with former holdings in Lorraine organized the "Interest Group of Mines and Iron/Steelworks in Alsace-Lorraine," which was soon recognized as a negotiating partner by the interwar German government on matters of economic consequence with France.[36] In the wake of the Nazi seizure of power in 1934, the consortium released a memorandum on the "squandering" of German mining and processing assets in France. It attributed the vulnerable dependence on imported ore in the interwar period to the loss of Germany's richest ore-producing regions after World War I, a factor contributing to the uncompetitively high cost of German pig iron and raw steel. The memorandum concluded by arguing that "a large part of the present superiority of the western European iron industries over the German is based upon the removal through the Versailles Treaty of the ore fields and steelworks, and their incorporation into an economic sphere opposed to Germany."[37] While stopping short of demanding proactive measures to recover the losses, the memorandum unambiguously tied German strategic vulnerability to the loss of Lorraine and suggested that Germany could enjoy no future security without reestablishing control over that area.

By 1940, the VSt had become the most noteworthy firm to advance claims on industrial assets in areas formerly governed by Germany. The interest of the VSt is expressed poignantly in a May 1940 exchange between Ernst Poensgen and a senior state secretary in the Economics Ministry. Referring principally to steel-producing works in Luxemburg, Poensgen noted that the firms that had founded the VSt had earlier constructed virtually the entire steel industry in the ore basin and retained control of it until the Versailles settlement. Referring to the strong possibility, widely discussed in industrial circles at the time, that state-appointed temporary commissioners or trustees would be appointed to manage the plants in the interest of the war economy, Poensgen insisted on preference being given to personnel from the VSt, "as [the steelworks] were taken from our ranks, and especially as the men who earlier ran the works are in part still in our service."[38] Poensgen referred in this connection chiefly to the Belwal and Differdingen works in Luxemburg and the Hagendingen works in Lorraine, which had belonged before 1918 to the Thyssen group, certain parts of which had folded into the VSt.[39] Poensgen argued that a decision to offer control of those works to other concerns would be unpardonable, regardless of where the concern in question was geographically situated. He included this last point presumably against the steel firms of the Saar, which had come to view the industry of Lorraine as within their natural sphere of influence. Poensgen forwarded his comments to Albert Vögler, then acting as deputy chairman of the VSt supervisory board, and to Otto Steinbrinck, who by that point had fallen out with Friedrich Flick and become a senior member of the VSt supervisory board. As events developed, Poensgen moderated his demands, promising that the VSt would not push for expropriations during the war but urging that observers from the concern be installed to oversee those plants it claimed.[40] The reasons for his moderation most probably lay in Poensgen's recognition that the structure of the steel industry had changed enough in the intervening time that the steel assets of Lorraine could not be distributed on the basis of previous ownership alone.

As the example of VSt suggests, private industry approached the question of industrial expropriation in Lorraine with a number of interrelated priorities. The chief objective was a distribution of property consistent with the maintenance of a stable set of relations among the major producers. As the umbrella organization of the German steel industry put it, each German concern should receive a proportion of the assets approximating its market share within the industry as a whole.[41] Fulfillment of that objective was complicated by the fact that different priorities motivated German steel firms to seek assets in Lorraine. Access to ore reserves solely implied an intention to supply furnaces in the Ruhr, but desire to expand productive capacity implied the acquisition of self-supplied plants in Lorraine. Only self-supplied plants or plants situated in the vicinity of mine heads offered a means of circumventing what had become the inefficiencies of the transportation network, so the competition for the processing mills themselves promised to be intense. The eventual political and legal status of the region was also a strong conditioning factor, as no industrialist relished the thought of acquiring and running steel firms in Lorraine under legally ambiguous terms. The only apparent certainty on which industrialists could rely was that Lorraine, particularly the heavily Germanized eastern districts, would eventually be incorporated into a future German Reich.

Assuming that the regime defined the legal and political parameters of doing business in Lorraine, German steel industrialists could anticipate substantial up-front expenses in acquiring the assets there. The plants in Lorraine had by all accounts suffered damage in the campaign, some quite heavily. French military engineers had in certain instances set explosives in the hope of rendering the plants unusable.[42] Reconstruction required trained personnel and plenty of transport resources, both in short supply.[43] Because French technical staff had fled before the advancing German armies, German firms in Lorraine also required skilled industrial engineers to restart the plants, which most German firms could ill afford to spare. Moreover, the Lorraine plants were technologically and structurally outdated relative to their German counterparts and would probably require massive investment to bring them up to a comparable standard.[44] As Hermann Röchling observed in 1941, the French had done precious little to stay current with the latest trends in the industry; one found in Lorraine, among other technological antiquities, the oldest Thomas steel processor on the continent.[45]

The most immediate obstacle to acquisitions in Lorraine by private German firms was to be found at the highest levels. The positions assumed by the two principal elements within the Nazi regime responsible for economic questions were not always apparent: the Economics Ministry, which was nominally responsible for governing the process of expansion and coordination, and the Four-Year Plan, which, through the Reichswerke, had a strong interest in protecting and expanding its authority relative to private industry and in seizing its own share of the spoils. As head of the Four-Year Plan, Hermann Göring reserved the right to authorize all acquisitions of industrial property in the newly conquered territories, citing the need to coordinate at the highest level such sensitive issues as capital transfers and foreign-exchange rights vis-à-vis interested third parties, such as the United States. In the event that foreign shareholders could not be persuaded to sell, Göring proposed crafting legal ownership provisions so onerous as to undermine any real control they retained over the assets in question, at least until those states became enemies of the Reich.[46]

Göring's willingness to assert the sovereignty of the Nazi regime over economic affairs and run roughshod over the legal rights of foreign owners clearly left most industrialists apprehensive, however much those rights may complicate their ability to acquire assets. Not much imagination was required to recognize that little more than legal convention stood between their own assets and a regime that gave such short shrift to notional property rights. The Economics Ministry, under the overall control of Walther Funk, represented the most supportive of official organs in relations with private industry and arguably possessed both the administrative scope and technical competence required to influence economic affairs more responsibly than Hitler's more fervent party loyalists. In a key position was a senior undersecretary in the Economics Ministry, General Hermann von Hanneken, who coordinated the overall system of administration of the German iron and steel industry through a dual appointment typical of the Nazi economic polycracy.[47] In addition to his ministerial posting, Göring appointed him general plenipotentiary for iron and steel in the Four-Year Plan organization, a post designed to reconcile possible conflicts involving steel issues between Göring's sprawling empire and the official state bureaucracy. Hanneken was in a prime position to influence the distribution of Lorraine assets among the interested German parties, even if he was ultimately constrained to act in accordance with Göring's wishes.

Plainly, the chief priority of Nazi policy in 1940 was to bring the steel plants of conquered Western Europe into operation as quickly as possible and in a manner least wasteful of limited resources.[48] On this score, industrialists moved quickly to clarify the collective position of the private sector and then to express the wishes of the major players in it. Even as the German military campaign against France was under way in 1940, the so-called Small Circle of major German industrialists, an informal convocation of the directors or owners of the leading firms, convened in Düsseldorf to discuss the status of the steel assets in eastern France and Luxemburg.[49] Flick, Poensgen, Vögler, Peter Klöckner, and others in the group acknowledged the need for a unified front to counter what they saw as the relentless advance of the Reichswerke, which they had little doubt would move quickly to seize the choicest spoils, just as it had in Austria, the Sudentenland, the Protektorat of Bohemia and Moravia, and most recently in Poland. The Reichswerke made early overtures toward the choicest steelworks in Lorraine and Luxemburg, including one of the largest works in Europe, de Wendel, which would give it between one-fifth and one-sixth of all French steel.[50] The acquisition program of the Reichswerke eventually expanded by 16 July to include the works of Hagendingen, Homecourt, and Arbed as well.[51]

The economics minister anticipated a conflict and sought to head off potential pretexts for it, at least on the side of private industry. In an effort to protect private industry against allegations of inappropriately monopolistic behavior, Funk had earlier issued a warning through the head of the industry's main interest group, the Reichsgruppe Industrie, to the effect that hasty demands for acquisitions in the newly occupied industrial regions could complicate a settlement with France and undermine the standing of private industry in official circles.[52] In his suspicion of private industry's desire for ambitious acquisition, Funk was surpassed by Göring, who issued a blanket prohibition on industrialists traveling through the newly occupied western territories on 20 June, arguing that their attempts to take over enterprises "must be rejected in the sharpest manner."[53]

The official admonitions had the desired effect, at least in the short term. The interest group chief, Wilhelm Zangen, encouraged his colleagues at the meeting of the "Small Circle" to suppress their desire for expropriation and work in the best interests of the nation as a whole.[54] Poensgen drafted a set of provisions on 24 June 1940 addressed to the Economics Ministry in which the industrialists pledged to refrain from asserting claims to the ore reserves and plants of eastern France until a peace settlement had been reached, on the condition that other interested parties, official or otherwise, likewise refrained.[55] With the conclusion of hostilities, the industrialists expected to regain control over the works they had previously owned, entirely or in part, prior to World War I. They foresaw that any remaining assets would be operated on the basis of an ownership pool comprising German steel firms. From the perspective of industry, this represented a reasonable compromise position. As they could argue, private German capital had originally nurtured the steel industry in Lorraine, and it seemed appropriate that the works there would again pass into private hands in due course. The sensitivities of the political situation necessitated circumspection in asserting claims, which the large players were willing to demonstrate up to a point.

On the same day that his memo appeared, Poensgen held a conference on behalf of the Ruhr works with General von Hanneken. Poensgen assumed a sympathetic ear, since Hanneken was thought to be well disposed to the concerns of the steel industry. Surprisingly, Poensgen argued that in view of how long ago the region had passed into French hands and the attending circumstances, the major German steel firms could make no plausible legal demands on the steelworks of Lorraine and Luxemburg. However, a certain moral right to expropriation might apply. On the basis of Articles 74 and 243 of the Treaty of Versailles, the French government had sequestered the German works after World War I and replaced their managements with appointed administrations.[56] Private French firms then acquired the plants through long-term installment payments on a favorable financial basis.[57] Compensation to the former German owners amounted to a paltry 6 to 10 percent of the actual value of the plants. A reciprocal right to expropriation therefore might apply under the circumstance of the German victory in 1940.[58] Certainly a strong moral case could be made for returning of Karlshütte to Hermann Röchling, from whose family the French government had summarily taken the plant in 1919. The Weimar government had eventually compensated Röchling with 10 percent of the plant's value, leaving him bitter and eager for redress.[59]

Even Poensgen's measured initiatives were too insistent for Hanneken. In a meeting with Flick's deputy Odilo Burkart in mid-June, the general averred that he would not tolerate a lengthy struggle over the industrial assets in Lorraine, a prospect not apparent in the calls by industry to that point, and that no arrangements would be determined until the war was over.[60] A practical view of Germany's needs supported this, given that a bitter squabble over control could undermine the regime's need to restart production in the occupied territories. In seeking to suppress claims for an indeterminate length of time, Hanneken could safely assume a conflict with the steel industrialists, who most probably favored a distribution sooner rather than later. Popular sentiment widely anticipated a quick end to the war, which to the industrial community implied less state management of the economy and a return to the comfortable export-oriented priorities of peacetime.[61] Evidence that heavy industry both hoped for and predicted a quick distribution of property is apparent in a memorandum circulated by the general secretary of the Economic Group of Iron and Steel Industry, Jacob Wilhelm Reichert, nearly a week before the armistice between Germany and France. In the memorandum he expressed the hope for a quick peace that would recast economic arrangements in Europe in Germany's favor. To that end, Reichert encouraged the recipients of the memorandum to consider losses they had incurred in 1919 and to advance claims on the basis of Germany's victory over France.[62] The sooner the regime arranged a peace with France, therefore, the sooner the process of taking over the industrial assets in the new territories could get under way.

Almost concurrent with the circulation of his memorandum, Reichert felt it worthwhile to issue a statement of private industry's position on the final status of the German position in Lorraine. In a speech before senior naval officers, Reichert explained that the construction of a steel industry up to the demands of the war required the complete integration into the Reich of the ore and steel plants in the new territories. He made clear that the assimilation of Lorraine and Luxemburg would serve as the foundation of the future German steel industry, which would derive its strength from its geographic scope.[63] Reichert reinforced this argument in the introduction to a major industry study, arguing that "concerns over a sufficient ore base have been surmounted now that the Lorraine-Luxemburg ore basin has fallen into our hands. The German people has its Führer Adolf Hitler, Field Marshall Hermann Göring and our military to thank for this major accomplishment."[64] The study underscored the fundamental improvement in Germany's economic prospects on the basis of its rich new ore supply. The ore fields of Lorraine, Luxemburg, and southern Belgium together contained an impressive 11 billion tons of ore, of which some 7 billion were readily extractable, a reserve so vast as to provide not only for the war effort, but as the foundation for the German economy far into the future.

Lurking behind such official pronouncements lay a more subtle rationale for private industry's eagerness to exploit the ore fields and steel mills of Lorraine, namely, that doing so undermined any reasonable argument in favor of ongoing state-sponsored initiatives to exploit low-grade domestic ores, thereby arguing against further expansion of the Reichswerke if not a complete abandonment of that enterprise.[65] With such a plentiful supply of inexpensive ore situated so close to the processing centers of the Ruhr, moreover, the steel industry would have the wherewithal to undertake a rationalization of its production processes and enhance its international competitiveness. Assuming that the assets found their way into the right hands, German industry would oversee resources on the basis of which, as Flick put it, "the lowest steel prime-costs in the world are secure."[66]

The efforts of private industrialists to acquire assets in the occupied western territories unfolded in the context of official measures to organize the economy there. In accord with the Wehrmacht order of June 1940 regulating the administration of captured enemy industrial properties, Hanneken appointed two commissioners for the iron and steel industry with the sanction of the Supreme Command. Otto Steinbrinck, Flick's chief deputy and most trusted agent until their rift in 1940, was placed in charge of the regions of Belgium, northern France, Luxemburg, and Longwy-Ardennes, while Hermann Röchling assumed control over Lorraine and the area around Meurthe-Moselle.[67] Formally, Röchling represented not just the German corporate community but the interest of the civil administrator, Bürckel. Consistent with that arrangement, rents received from the operation of the plants were deposited into special restricted accounts, and leases to run the plants were negotiated not with former owners but through the authorities. Notwithstanding the appointments of Steinbrinck and Röchling, private industry subsequently showed awareness that decisions regarding the distribution of assets actually rested with the Reich leadership, no doubt as a result of how contentious the distribution process became. Whatever the extent of Röchling's authority in the matter, his appointment ensured a conflict of interest, as he had strong claims on certain steel firms in the region under his supervision.

Among those vying for an advantaged position in the distribution of industrial spoils in Lorraine, none considered himself more deserving than the ardently right-wing Hermann Röchling, widely considered the leading heavy industrialist of the Saar region.[68] Röchling rose to political prominence in industrial circles through his demands for expansive annexations in World War I, in part due to the extensive historical connections between the heavily industrialized regions of eastern France and the part of Germany in which his own plants lay. After the loss of the war in 1918, Röchling struggled to reestablish a supply of ore for his iron and steel plants, refusing to reconcile himself to the permanent separation of Lorraine from the Reich.[69] The Saar region itself, moreover, fell under an interim French occupation authority after 1918, not to be reunited with Germany until a 1935 plebiscite. During the occupation the economic affairs of the Saar were integrated even more deeply with those of France and particularly Alsace-Lorraine.[70] Production in Röchling's two flagship steelworks fell markedly relative to the other thirteen large German firms, and Röchling's voice in industrial policy waned with the decline of his economic fortunes. With the partition from the Reich and loss of its ore supply, the economic significance of the Saarland steadily declined against that of the Ruhr. The failure or inability of Röchling to consolidate and rationalize his plants in a manner similar to the industry at large only abetted his marginalization after the Saar rejoined Germany in 1935, at which point the costs of his inputs soared.[71]

Röchling's adamantly right-wing political views resonated strongly with the new civil administration in Lorraine after 1940 and probably accounted for his appointment as commissioner for sequestered properties there. As a further measure, the Nazi civil administrator for Lorraine,

Bürckel, named Röchling to the position of special representative for the mines and works of Lorraine, an arrangement approved by Hanneken and confirmed subsequently by Göring in his role as director of the Four-Year Plan organization.[72] Röchling's appointment was not unopposed. The Flick concern attempted in late June 1940 to force the appointment of its own candidate, Rudolf Brenneke, through the machinations of a junior official in the Economics Ministry.[73] Brenneke was an old Lorraine hand, having worked in the steel industry for more than twenty years before ending up as general director of the Kneuttingen works. The Flick concern's contact in the ministry demurred, however, pointing out that Brenneke was somewhat advanced in years, and indicated that Göring preferred Röchling for unclear reasons. Flick was informed that the most he could hope to secure for Brenneke was a deputy plenipotentiary position.[74] Given the advanced age and marginal status of his candidate, however, it seems clear that Flick's concern did not consider the issue to be of great importance.

Bürckel's apparent motivation in naming Röchling was to ensure that the final disposition of economic resources in Lorraine reinforced his power and authority as civil administrator and Gauleiter. Almost immediately, he charged Röchling with preparing a confidential report on the ownership arrangements of the major Lorraine steelworks. The report would presumably buttress Bürckel's declared sovereign authority to define the future shape of property relations in his domain. Merely to assert such authority placed him in almost certain conflict with Hanneken, who appears to have intended to use his influence with Göring to have the latter open the region to steel concerns without a historic claim in the region or foothold in the Saar. For his part, Bürckel had already issued a statement identifying the most important Lorraine steel firms and establishing guidelines for their orderly transition into German hands.[75] Along those same lines, Rochling's report reflected Bürckel's desire to exclude the largest German iron and steel concerns, based predominantly in the Ruhr, in favor of those based in the Saar. The text stipulated that former French owners were to be prevented from holding even minority stakes in the recollectivized firms, that former ownership arrangements should not define the apportionment of property, and that the ore in Lorraine was to be used firstly to cover the supply requirements of the Saar, with the concerns of the Ruhr having access only to whatever remained.[76] The last point in Röchling's report must have appeared preposterous to steel industrialists, as common sense suggested that the foundries in the Saar could never absorb more than a minute fraction of the ore in Lorraine without a massive expansion of their capacity, something the regime and the rest of industry were highly unlikely to finance.

The mainstream reply to Röchling's report lacked the force of its convictions. Hanneken tasked Poensgen with preparing his own comprehensive assessment of the steel plants in Lorraine and Luxemburg along with recommendations for their distribution among the major German firms. However, Poensgen lacked Röchling's passion for the issue and shied from the assignment. Preferring to avoid what he apparently considered to be a political minefield, he produced a report merely detailing the ownership arrangements in place before 1914. Unsatisfied with Poensgen's reluctance to assume even an indirect stand on the issue of redistribution, Hanneken demanded an advisory report based not only on previous arrangements but on a survey of the current constellation of ownership in the steel industry, which included a host of players absent before 1918, including Flick and the Reichswerke. Poensgen demurred again, preferring instead to establish a commission consisting of himself, Reichert, and two minor officials to collect the required materials and process the recommendations through the Small Circle of major Ruhr industrialists.[77] The reasons for Poensgen's delay lay most plausibly in a desire to receive clearer statements of intent from the other large steel producers and to gauge the reaction of the authorities to an informal expression of their demands. Therefore, aside from Röchling's report and the industry general study earlier completed under Reichert's supervision, a comprehensive assessment of the industrial assets in Lorraine and a recommendation for their distribution would have to issue from other sources.

By mid-1940 it was apparent to German industrialists and policymakers alike that the rich ore fields of Lorraine presented remarkable opportunities for addressing some of the most critical problems thought to be confronting the German mobilization effort. The industrial community viewed the resources of the region as central to the war effort and the long-term predominance of the German economy in Europe. Private industry expressed its first tentative preferences for a distribution of the assets in the occupied western territories based in part on historical affiliations, especially in the case of the steel industry of the Saar and the traditional firms of the Ruhr. But the shape of the German steel industry had changed in the years since 1919 and the demands of a figure like Friedrich Flick, who had assembled his empire in the interwar period and was in a position to air his demands in the most influential quarters, would factor decisively in the outcome.

Chapter 4

Friedrich Flick's Campaign to Acquire the Rombach Works, 1940–1944

The German victory over France in June 1940 initiated a scramble for the resources of Lorraine within the German steel industry and an effort to define and execute a coherent approach to the distribution of assets within the Nazi regime. Few, if any, doubted that Germany was wholly entitled to Lorraine and the economic assets in it. For Flick, German dominion over the region was an irresistible temptation to augment his holdings at the expense of interwar French owners.[1] After the Aryanization campaign of the previous years and the ethical and legal challenges it posed, the prospect of acquiring properties in a conquered territory like Lorraine presented no dilemmas other than how to outmaneuver other interested parties, a game at which Flick was by now adept. His failure to participate successfully in the takeover of industrial assets in other recently conquered parts of Europe—Austria, the Sudetenland, or in the rump territories of Czechoslovakia generally—provided additional motivation to pursue the great prizes in the eastern French mining districts. The Reichswerke had shown itself willing to move forcefully into new areas and push out private competition, raising the stakes for men like Flick and presenting a difficult new challenge to their calculations.

In surveying the political landscape in the newly occupied regions of Western Europe, Flick could draw on the confusion that seemed to define so much Nazi administration. The arrangements developed to manage the economic affairs of the region, outlined in previous chapters, strongly reflected the disjointed character of Nazi governance generally.[2] Despite Göring's nominal status as the supreme coordinator of Germany's war economy at home and in the lands of the growing German empire, numerous other coordinative bodies—the Economics Ministry, regional administrators, and industrial interest organizations—moved aggressively in 1940 to stake out spheres of influence. They need not necessarily have contended directly with Göring or challenged his ability to issue binding orders to be effective; Göring's own lack of rigorous economic knowledge and notoriously short attention span,[3] as well as the dispersed character of power generally in the Third Reich, combined to ensure that ambitious subordinates and industrialists retained ample space to shape economic relations in a manner more or less consistent with their parochial concerns.

The steel firm in Lorraine that became the focus of Flick's attention, Rombach, had been founded originally in 1881 by a German industrial magnate. The first blast furnace became active in 1890, the first steel-works were opened in 1900, and an ore-smelting plant in nearby Machern was acquired in 1905.[4] At the end of World War I the plant passed into French hands. The French government confiscated the physical plant and its supporting ore mines under Articles 74 and 243 of the Versailles Treaty, along with the rest of the German steel industry of the region. The Société Lorraine des Aciéries de Rombas, the French holding company in possession of the works in 1940, had been founded in November 1919 by the French industrial group Laurent expressly to take over and manage the Rombach works.[5] A consortium of leading French steel firms capital-ized the new venture with 150 million francs and founded a new corpora-tion to operate it.[6] The firm included the mines of Rombach, Sainte-Marie, and Rosselange encompassing an area of 1,764,645 hectares and containing some 150 millions tons of iron ore.[7] The coke supply derived largely from sources in northern France and Belgium, amounting to roughly 45,000 tons of coke for every 140,000 tons of ore processed into iron. The steel-works included eight blast furnaces with a daily production of 220 to 380 tons of cast iron, a Thomas steelworks, a Martin steelworks, an electrical steelworks, and ten rolling mills. It also included a steel plant with four blast furnaces in nearby Mézières-les Metz.

By 1940, the condition of the plant had declined steeply. A commis-sion of German experts tasked with assessing the value of the Lorraine steel industry rated the technological state of the works to be high relative to other works in Lorraine, but low relative to those in Germany proper. According to German appraisers, the interwar owners opted to siphon off the proceeds from their low-cost production instead of investing to bring the works up to the standard of international competitiveness.[8]

Its condition notwithstanding, Rombach represented an impressive prospect for Flick. Under optimal conditions the total production of the firm amounted to roughly a million tons of steel per year, approximating some 8 percent of the total production of the entire French industry.[9] The firm also controlled shares in a number of other operations in the interest of securing necessary production inputs as well as safe outlets for its products.[10] It therefore enjoyed well-established market connections for its products in France, important when one considered the contiguous character of the economic area likely to result from Nazi plans for the postwar European economy. The largest drawback was the high cost of coking coal in Lorraine, easily the most expensive input in the production process.[11] Without a reliable and inexpensive source of coke, the comparative advantages enjoyed by the Lorraine works would be greatly reduced and the plant would not long survive in an environment of full utilization and fierce competition for inputs. An official report detailing the state of the steel industry in Lorraine had earlier dealt with this vulnerability. The Economics Ministry established an industry commission on 21 February 1941 to assess the value of the plants based on the physical assets and their likely productive capacity under the most probable future circumstances.[12] The conclusions reached by the experts appointed to the commission affirmed that the great advantage of the steel industry in Lorraine lay in its exceptionally low "Selbtskosten," meaning the cost to the firm itself of a ton of finished steel, based on ready and inexpensive access to ore inputs controlled for the most part by the plants themselves. Based on the structure of the industry in Lorraine, the commission assigned to Rombach a value of RM 23 million, a figure described by one economic official as a lowball estimate favorable to Flick.[13]

As pointed out in the previous chapter, in early July 1940 the mines under Rombach's control became the responsibility of Paul Raabe as general representative for iron and ore production on behalf of the Economics Ministry, responsible for the region of Mosel, in which the Rombach mines figured prominently. They remained under his supervision until the liberation in 1944. Hermann Röchling assumed initial control of the actual plants in his capacity as general representative for iron and steel, although he installed a deputy to manage Rombach on-site. On 5 July, Röchling issued guidelines defining the responsibilities and conduct of German officials assigned to operate the facilities before trustee firms could be appointed.[14] Among other provisions, the guidelines specifically forbade French owners and directors from entering the factories and demanded that they remand any funds with which they may have absconded for paying off back wages, many of the French executives apparently having done precisely that.

While the ad hoc German economic administration took the first steps toward assessing the value of the plants and renewing production, Flick began to work behind the scenes to acquire a share of the spoils for himself. After participating in the June 1940 meeting at which the major figures in the steel industry resolved to refrain from asserting immediate claims, Flick left Düsseldorf to take the thermal baths in Marienbad. From there he drafted a memorandum to Ernst Buskühl, general director of the Harpen coal works and one of his chief confidants. The memorandum detailed Flick's decision to go after the Rombach steelworks and sketched a strategy to close out challengers and win over the authorities. Flick opened with a disclaimer, arguing that the then-prevailing circumstances were hardly optimal for commercial transactions, but that the enormous implications of the war for the future structure of the German steel industry demanded a proactive approach to acquisitions in the new territories. Without doubt, he reasoned, the industry of the conquered Lorraine-Luxemburg regions would become German and previous German owners would be entitled to the works they once controlled.[15] Flick was not the only party without prior claims on plants in Lorraine eager to find a footing there. The Reichswerke intended to bid for de Wendel and Havendingen, so Flick reckoned that only Arbed and Rombach would be left without claimants. Arbed was probably too sweet a prize, so Flick intended to assert what he called a strong "moral claim" to Rombach, namely that he was entitled to a prize in Lorraine by virtue of having earlier given up large and productive coalfields to the Reichswerke. The Reichswerke had justified its demand for these concessions with the argument that as the second-largest producer of coal in the West, Flick enjoyed a coal surplus too substantial for internal demand to absorb. Flick intended to point out that every major Rheinisch-Westfälische concern had refused to surrender coal mines to the Reichswerke because its steel operations consumed virtually the entire supply. The surrender had been against his better judgment and turned out to be a loss-generator for his concern. Thus, Flick could make a strong claim that he had extended a helping hand to the Reichswerke when other major industrialists had refused, and that as a supporter of this Nazi venture he deserved some consideration in the apportionment of spoils in return.

The situation on the ground in Lorraine bore out Flick's prediction that coking coal would be a prime determinant in official deliberations. The general shortage of coking coal throughout the steel industry promised to worsen as the Lorraine works were brought on line, since the regular sources of French and Belgian coke had become unavailable. Problems throughout the industry in Lorraine became apparent soon after the German military campaign in 1940. Monthly coke supply requirements for the region in November, for example, amounted to nearly 200,000 tons; the interim economic authorities allotted only 155,000 tons to cover that demand, but transport difficulties that month, a wholly typical one, ensured that only 58 percent of the allotment reached its destination.[16] Given the fair assumption that Flick had to have been aware of the worsening supply situation, one must question Flick's stated "conclusion that the Rombacher Steelworks . . . is a suitable property for Harpen," at least under the circumstances prevailing in 1940.[17] No amount of surplus coking coal in his operations in the Altreich could guarantee that a plant he acquired in Lorraine would be sufficiently supplied, only that it would enjoy a privileged claim on the coke reserves in his concern. Of course, Flick may not have foreseen the widening of the war to include a crusade against the Soviet Union a year later, nor anticipated what effect this, as well as the German declaration of war on the United States in December 1941, would have on his ability to take over and profitably operate a steel plant in Lorraine. And neither Flick nor anyone else could accurately foresee how difficult it would be to maintain the transportation system over the longer term. He certainly cannot be faulted for making his bid on Rombach on the basis of the structural compatibility that clearly obtained between it and Harpen.

The compatibilities between the two firms had long been apparent to officials from each. As Flick pointed out in his memorandum to Buskühl, Rombach and Harpen had actually explored the possibility of a formal pact before World War I, with each sending leading members of their supervisory boards to assess the operations and facilities of the other.[18] Despite loose affiliations with various west German steel firms for the purpose of gaining access to coking coal, Rombach never formally combined with a German counterpart and no legal German shareholders sat on the sidelines awaiting a slice of the ownership. However, Rombach had been closer to Harpen than any other German firm. With an eye to having Harpen become the chief institutional shareholder in Rombach, Flick suggested that Harpen should perhaps shed its long-standing identity as a pure coal firm and diversify vertically into steel production. He claimed to have drawn inspiration in this connection from reading a biography of the German industrialist Emil Kirdorf, which described the latter's opportune affiliation of his mining operations with downstream smelting plants at that moment when syndicate agreements conferring special rights to "mixed enterprises" were renewed in the early years of the century, a bold move based apparently on the great industrialist's intuitive grasp of market possibilities. Flick's own intuition suggested that the structure of the industry was shifting decisively and the time was ripe for just a similarly daring stroke. The war launched by the Nazi state would fundamentally recast European economic relations and shake up the German steel industry.

As for financing, Flick envisaged that Harpen would join with his hard-coal operation, Essener Steinkohle, to finance the purchase of Rombach from the German authorities over a period of four to five years through cash surpluses or tax-free amortizations, with the goal of raising RM 12–15 million annually for new installations. Time precluded putting together a financing scheme of greater sophistication. Pursuing this program implied a drastic reconfiguration of his concern: "If I assume that a sum of 30 million cash Reichmarks would have to be raised to acquire Rombach, which includes 20 million that I intend to borrow, then I see no other solution but that Harpen should forfeit its role in the brown coal concern. Whether the Mittelstahl group could assume control of the whole thing, I cannot judge at the moment."[19] At 30 percent greater than the early official assessed value of the Klein Commission, Flick's own estimation of the likely costs proved high; whether the differences reflected intentional undervaluation by the regime or a tendency by Flick to assess his prospects pessimistically is unclear. At the very least, one can point out that the lower assessed value by the official commission undoubtedly eased the debt load Flick shouldered to finance his acquisition.

Flick's lengthy memorandum to Buskühl revealed arguments to be marshaled for the authorities, but little in the way of the underlying motives that brought about his desire to expand his operations westward. Only after the war did he reveal his true purposes. In testimony at his trial for war crimes, he distinguished between motives officially offered and those that remained unarticulated until the war was over.[20] The prime motive for Flick's decision to pursue Rombach was in the growing power of the Reichswerke, which had acquired by that point the last independent Bavarian steelworks, the Luitpoldhütte, had broken ground on a massive new steel mill in the east, and had set about taking over the lion's share of the steel industry in Lorraine and Luxemburg. This expansion threatened to crush Flick's Maxhütte works in central Germany "between [the] two millstones" of the Reichswerke, namely Linz in the east and the operations in Lorraine in the west. Given its vulnerable position in that contingency, Flick foresaw an eventual assimilation of Maxhütte as well. The best strategy, he reasoned, was to carry the fight to the Reichswerke by acquiring a sizable holding in Lorraine, thereby reinforcing the competitive position of his concern and perhaps even laying the groundwork for an accord with the Reichswerke on sales and production matters. Flick recalled that prior to 1918, the Lorraine works had marketed a large share of their output in southern Germany, a situation he expected to resume with the return of peacetime conditions.[21] Moreover, the probable acquisition by the Reichswerke of extensive steel operations in Lorraine promised to increase its appetite for coal to fuel them: "That was one of the reasons why we took the standpoint that it would be better for us to find a consumer of our own, a new large-scale coal consumer."[22]

Flick's postwar account complicates the historical reconstruction of his motives. While not invalidating his arguments for acquisition based on his "moral claim" or the suitability of a tighter compact between Harpen

and Rombach, his more forthright acknowledgment of the strongly political character of economic logic in the Third Reich makes his campaign
seem like a conscientious effort to fortify his corporate position against the
growing economic reach of the Nazi state.

Given his experience by this point, Flick's strategy for acquiring
Rombach required an approach to the Reich economic bureaucracy far
less sophisticated than had been necessary for his acquisitions of the
1930s, especially the Petschek properties. Petitioning for control of property dubbed by the regime as spoils of war potentially involved fewer legal
gymnastics and presumably less inhumanity than removing property from
Jewish persons only recently stripped of their legal standing.

The first step involved sounding out the Flick concern's contacts in the
upper reaches of the Reich economics bureaucracy. On 10 June 1940 Odilo
Burkart, Flick's principal deputy for steel questions, held a conference with
General Hermann von Hanneken, the Economics Ministry official responsible for the steel industry. Hanneken was mistrustful of Burkart, describing him to his staff as the person sent by Flick as a "bloodhound" to sniff
out officials in advance on delicate questions and admonishing them to
be careful in his presence.[23] Perhaps because he guarded his words carefully when speaking with Burkart, Hanneken assumed a moderate position
toward the acquisition of works in the occupied territories.[24] He made it
clear that the Economics Ministry exercised final responsibility for bringing the inoperative works in Lorraine into line with the war economy. Only
after the war would he consider questions of transferring legal ownership
of the steel plants, and then only after full consideration of previous ownership arrangements and for a fair market value. Hanneken considered the
ore resources in the occupied West in a similar light, drawing a distinction
between those affiliated with specific steelworks and "free pits," the product
of which he advocated pooling for the benefit of the entire German steel
industry. On the latter point Hanneken must have expected to incur the dis-
approval of the leaders of the German steel industry, who could point out
that the only advantage to operating works in Lorraine lay in their access
to a virtually unlimited supply of cheap ore, and would be reluctant to see
that access denied in favor of communal allotments. Regardless, Hanneken
preferred to postpone a solution to these distributional problems until later.

In his proclaimed desire to oversee a fair market allocation of the assets and a partial collectivization of the resource base in Lorraine, he could not be counted on to support Flick's bid for a share in the spoils there.

Like vultures circling a carcass, private industrialists were not going to wait for the approval of the regime before asserting their claims. On 26 June 1940 Jakob Wilhelm Reichert, the secretary of the Economic Group Iron Producing Industry, circulated to its chief members a memorandum from the *Reichsgruppe Industrie*. The memorandum requested, on behalf of the Reich government, that the industrialists consider a program of acquisition in the occupied western territories in the light of the pending peace treaty and reconfiguration of economic relations in Europe. Reichert specifically requested not detailed and lengthy studies, but brief drafts to be submitted by 1 July 1940 as a beginning point for more substantial deliberations later. The territories he asked the firms to consider were vast and provide a sense of how expansive were future German economic ambitions: Norway, Denmark, Sweden, Finland, Holland, Belgium, Luxemburg, France, England, and the Balkans. The terms under which steel firms were to advance their claims were equally expansive: the industrialists were to consider losses of virtually any kind they had suffered under the Versailles Treaty, but more importantly, what specific broader measures and reforms of an official nature they wished to see instituted in the "new European economic structure" of the future.[25] Reichert's request may be interpreted variously. On the corporate side, some systematic response to the new economic framework in which Nazi expansion had placed German firms seemed unavoidable. On the official side, a request for an overview of corporate demands for acquisition neither implied a desire on the part of the authorities to reshape future European economic arrangements in a manner consistent with the interests of private industry, nor bound the regime's planning agencies to any specific course in reviewing proposals for future arrangements. Reichert's request more probably reflected a perceived need for a more thorough understanding of the implications of an aggressive strategy of acquisition in the western territories and of which corporate parties had a stake in the outcome.

Clearly anticipating these initiatives, and either before his departure for Marienbad or during his visit there, Flick requested from Karl Raabe, the chief of his Maxhütte steel plant, a detailed assessment of the Rombach and Kneuttingen works, the latter of which he had indicated in his earlier brief would most likely be reserved for the Klöckner firm.[26] Flick's request is revealing. He either had not yet resolved to pursue Rombach exclusively or sought to backstop his push for a plant in the occupied West with a secondary bid for Kneuttingen. The latter possibility is the most likely, given the substance of his earlier strategic memorandum to Burkart, the superior condition and greater potential of the Rombach works, and the fact any bid for Kneuttingen would likely be contested bitterly by the Klöckner firm, which could assert a claim based on prior ownership. In any case, not having seen either plant for more than two decades, Raabe apparently relied on a secondhand source in compiling his two-page report for Flick, although the source in question, the Demag industrial works, was well informed enough to have acquired detailed intelligence about Rombach's extensive renovations in the interwar period. Raabe's evaluation of the plants and their equipment reveals their potential value and Flick's decision to pursue Rombach.

At the outset, Raabe deemed Kneuttingen a substandard operation that had seen no improvement in the interwar period and was probably not worth Flick's consideration. Rombach came off much more favorably. Raabe described Rombach's usual monthly output of raw steel at its height in World War I as between 50,000 and 60,000 tons, which accorded roughly with similar plants in Lorraine, Luxemburg, and the Saar. Both Rombach and Kneuttingen had blast furnace systems of similar quality, although Rombach had a Martin steelworks of three ovens, which enabled it to process its own scrap and achieve a greater cost efficiency. The most noteworthy distinction lay in a comparison of the rolling mills. Rombach was equipped with an integral and well-designed mill operation capable of producing several forms of finished steel, whereas the Kneuttingen facilities were scattered over a wide area and handicapped by outmoded apparatus. Based on this simple appraisal, Raabe concluded that Rombach was well outfitted and could be returned to full production relatively quickly, whereas Kneuttingen would likely require a renovation of its rolling mill operations to bring it up to a profitable standard.[27] How much Flick depended on Raabe's report, which was disseminated among the senior leadership of the concern, is open to question. Raabe himself had little motivation at the time to embellish the condition of the Rombach works, although it should be pointed out that Flick later appointed him to head it along with Flick's son, Otto-Ernst.

In the meantime, the official handling of the division of spoils in the occupied West had taken a beneficial turn for Flick. His chief deputy for steel issues, Burkart, had received a communication from Ernst Poensgen of the VSt clarifying the developing situation and hinting that Flick was a leading contender for a share in the spoils. The Economics Ministry official dealing with these issues, General von Hanneken, had earlier tasked Poensgen with developing a program for apportioning the steel assets in the occupied West among the major German producers. Before a recent conference with Flick's former associate Otto Steinbrinck, Poensgen had interpreted his task as consisting solely of documenting pre-Versailles ownership arrangements; he now understood that he was to advance more detailed proposals for a progressive distribution of property in the West among the current major steel concerns, particularly the Reichswerke, which obviously would not have figured in any ownership assessment of the period before 1918. Without any apparent prompting from Flick, Poensgen anticipated correctly that the latter probably had an acquisition strategy for the West and sought his input before submitting any further proposals. In his exchange with Poensgen, Burkart made no mention of Rombach, saying simply that Flick had "certain wishes" and requested what Poensgen had already affirmed, namely that he take no further step without first consulting Flick.[28]

As the deliberations of the major private industrialists accelerated, the official organs of the Nazi regime undertook their own preliminary assessment of the plants in Lorraine. On 26 July 1940, the Reichstelle für Eisen und Stahl, a supervisory office in the Economics Ministry for the iron and steel industry, issued a major report outlining a framework for the distribution of the major works in Luxemburg and Lorraine including Longwy, Briey, and Nancy, which together possessed a monthly productive capacity of some 1.1 million tons of pig iron.[29] The report specifically included works not earlier controlled by Germans but in the contiguous ore belt of those regions. In framing its recommendations the authors of the report considered four key conditions, all of which undoubtedly seemed, given the circumstances, eminently reasonable: pre–World War I owner-ship arrangements, the relationship between the coal supply of the major German concerns and their raw iron output, the reconcilability of pro-ductive programs between German firms and the targeted properties, and the benefits of maintaining established relations between firms in Lorraine after expropriation by different competing German firms. The report emphasized that prior ownership arrangements were not to determine the distribution entirely, else the VSt would benefit to an extent disruptive to the structure of the industry. Furthermore, consideration of the coal sup-plies of the major German firms was important, as it revealed that those firms in a position to make the most compelling claims based on prior ownership, especially VST and Klöckner, had very tight coal bases and could not supply their own operations from internal resources.[30] Beyond that, however, the problem of reconciling the productive programs of the Lorraine and German works was important in only marginal cases, and then only because certain major works in Luxemburg and Lorraine had integrated rolling mill operations. Finally, the report pointed to the eco-nomic and technical collaboration that had developed over time among some of the firms in Lorraine, especially the five components of the vast Arbed concern. Disruption of those patterns stood to undercut the finan-cial or industrial efficiencies to be had by distributing them among differ-ent German firms.

The report defined the ultimate purpose of expropriation as a distri-bution of property consistent with the maintenance of a stable set of rela-tions among the producers, or a distribution whereby major concerns would receive apportionments roughly proportional to their current share of total capacity. In other words, the authors of the ministry report did not view the works in Lorraine as an economic weapon to be used to the advantage of any single party. Certain qualifications were necessary: Krupp was already heavily invested in a major program of expansion in the east, while a prior wave of acquisitions by Mannesmann had led that company to abstain from further acquisitions for the time being.[31] Furthermore, the authorities had to pay careful attention to the technical and logistical ability of German firms to provide for the reconstruction and staffing of the expropriated assets, no mean task in a technical labor market already severely stretched by wartime requirements and shortages. Conferring a steel mill in Lorraine on a German firm that could neither supply it with the requisite coking coal nor staff it with the necessary personnel was not in the interest of the war economy.

The report by the Reichstelle appeared before intensive bargaining between interested firms and the Reich government had taken place. Interestingly, the report noted that the Flick concern had advanced no "direct claims" on industrial properties in the occupied West; it can thus be argued that any prescriptions advanced in the document resulted from rational appraisal of the advantages and disadvantages of a union between Flick and Rombach based on the needs of the war effort. Under the circumstances then prevailing and independent of Flick's own preferences, awarding Rombach to Flick was seen by key elements of the Reich bureaucracy as consistent with the regime's priorities of assimilating the sequestered Lorraine industries, bringing them into war production as quickly as possible, and doing so in a manner that maintained balance among the major producers in the steel industry.

That the Flick concern exerted influence over the authors of the ministry report is suggested by the presence in it of information proprietary to the concern and presumably made available to buttress arguments in its favor. The report cited the negotiations between Flick's Harpen group and Rombach prior to World War I as evidence of a basic compatibility between the two based on Harpen's substantial coal surplus and Rombach's need for a consistent coke supply, a connection that may well have provoked the report's association of the two firms. As additional grounds the report referred to the vulnerabilities of the Flick concern's heavy overall dependence on scrap metal as a primary input and the presumed benefits of diversifying the concern's raw materials base. A successful expropriation would increase the Flick concern's production of pig iron, which was disproportionately low relative to its output of raw steel by an estimated 20 percent.[32] Clearly, the report contained information of which the authors of the Reichstelle report could not have been aware without input from the Flick concern, which suggests that the latter had already begun to lobby official organs in advance of the formal process of bargaining. However, the material in the report about the Flick concern complemented arguments advanced about the state of the steel industry on a number of fronts, not all of them having to do with the concern.

Flick's other initiatives around this time confirm the existence of a behind-the-scenes campaign to line up support for his acquisition of Rombach. In early August, Bernhard Weiss, a general plenipotentiary of the Flick concern with responsibility for its hard-coal operation, instructed Burkart, Flick's principal deputy for steel questions, to apprise Ernst Poensgen of Flick's consultations with Mannesmann's Wilhelm Zangen on the issue of western expropriations. Both Flick and Zangen warned Poensgen not to be drawn into discussion of the issue with officials of the Krupp concern, pre-sumably in order to block competing claims. They also proposed that any scheme for paying for the expropriated works not distinguish between firms resuming control over earlier assets and those assuming control over new assets, which they interpreted inexplicably as a way of safeguarding the own-ership privileges of the former. Essentially, they anticipated a format whereby 50 percent of the asset's value would be disbursed immediately to the regime and the remaining half paid out in installments over a ten-year period.[33] Such a scheme was by no means even-handed. It would ensure that firms already over-leveraged as a result of the massive industrial expansion of the late 1930s would find it difficult to find the financial means to compete, and close out smaller firms for whom taking on such debt would be prohibitive. The evi-dence provides no indication as to why firms could not arrange financing on an individual basis, leading to the conclusion that Flick and Zangen sought through financing stipulations to delimit the number of firms qualified to participate in the scramble for spoils. Aside from reinforcing his already-established position against potential upstarts, however, it is unclear how such an arrangement favored the Flick concern specifically.

Key officials from the Flick concern devoted a major planning con-ference to the situation in Lorraine on 16 August to discussing their firm's steel operations and how its expropriation targets fit into them. Much of the material presented to the conference participants reaffirmed Raabe's earlier report to Flick on the Rombach works. The officials evaluated the critical issues of raw materials and logistical costs in a comparative light, the purpose being to grasp the implications of a successful acquisition of Rombach on the shape of the industry. They reiterated that the profitability of any acquisition in Lorraine would depend on a stable supply of ore to keep input costs down; Flick's technical experts reported on the basis of hearsay that each major firm in the minette basin would receive an ore-field allotment sufficient for seventy-five to eighty years, most probably from those holdings adjacent to the works themselves, with marginal adjustments to ensure that accidents of geography did not work to the disadvantage of other firms.[34]

In an assessment similar to those of Flick and Raabe earlier, the conference participants coolly determined that Rombach, in combination with a smaller plant at Homecourt, was the plant best suited to Flick's current and future profile within the industry, especially given its notional ability to produce multiple forms of semi-finished and finished steel. Moreover, strong practical objections were aired against attempting to gain control of other, putatively more desirable works. The Reichswerke was sure to snap up the largest prize, the de Wendel group and many subsidiaries, while a drive by Flick to acquire Differdingen would run counter to the prior ownership claims of the VSt (which could make a strong case for ownership through one of its founding firms). The question of a competent labor force, one of the single most critical issues confronting economic activity generally in Nazi Germany, had been little considered by Flick and his leading subordinates up to that point, and the conference did not treat the issue in depth. Participants appeared united in their belief that plants in the formerly German portion of Lorraine would prove much easier to man than those in the French areas, especially with skilled engineers, as a result of the presumed ethnic sentiments of the inhabitants, while a similarly positive labor outlook could be assumed for those firms interested in Luxemburg as well.[35] Strikingly absent is any reliable information about the actual sentiments of workers in the area or at the Rombach plant, as well as the larger question of what effects the ongoing war would have on its management or profitability.

Throughout the expropriation process, the question of French participation in the new ownership arrangements figured only marginally but remained a potentially sensitive point. The Nazi regime had still not negotiated a peace treaty with the Vichy government and no detailed conception of the future European economic order could be discerned amidst the dislocations of the war. An accommodating posture toward interwar French owners stood to foster the preconditions for the anticipated peace treaty and cultivate the cooperative economic relations thought to be desirable in future European economic relations. The possibility of French minority shareholding implied tapping French capital for ends defined and regulated by the Reich. It also implied the possibility of diversifying ownership in a manner presumably desirable to Nazi economic policymakers concerned with the scope and power of heavy industry. However, the industrial community expressed virtually unanimous opposition to the notion. Flick, in particular, was habitually disinclined to share control over his assets, as his early participation in the VSt well demonstrated. In notes prepared for a conference with Albert Vögler in July 1940, Flick referenced an idea advanced by General von Hanneken of the Economics Ministry that called for 20 to 25 percent French minority shareholding as "in my opinion not appropriate."[36]

For Hanneken, who by this point could be fairly seen as skeptical of the ambitions of private industry in the occupied areas, the unresolved problem of financing and what it entailed for ownership persisted. Indeed, this was among the chief points he raised in discussions with the Flick concern about expropriations. On 27 August 1940, Burkart argued in a remarkably frank exchange with Hanneken that virtually every interested governmental office agreed with Flick's "moral" claim to the Rombach plant in light of his loss of the Bismarckhütte in Upper Silesia. Hanneken, however, expressed bewilderment that Flick should want to expand westward when the most sensible direction of Mittelstahl's expansion from central Germany would be eastward into Silesia. To this point Burkart offered a threefold response. Mittelstahl's operations depended overly on scrap, and Flick wished to diversify its production through ore mining. Only in Lothringen was a secure and accessible domestic ore basis to be found. Morever, Flick's major colliery, Harpen, retained a remarkably large coke surplus relative to other firms and was perhaps the only source that could provide for Rombach adequately. It had already sacrificed some 30 percent of its coal reserves over the previous few years to the Reichswerke, and Flick wished to remove any pretext for surrendering additional assets for the greater good of the German war effort. When Hanneken again emphasized the value of looking east, Burkart brought up his third point, namely that the regime could depend only on concerns with substantial capital reserves to take over, renovate, and renew production in the Lorraine works, leaving unmentioned the possibilities open if alternative methods of financing were considered. Hanneken remarked acidly that what was happening in Lorraine was the same as what had already happened in Upper Silesia: the major producers were fighting viciously over the best prizes, leaving the remainder to be picked over "like sour beer." Burkart offered soothingly that the Flick concern did not wish for the Lorraine works to be given away, but purchased from the government at a fair value under "appropriate circumstances."[37]

Hanneken's opposition to Flick's campaign for Rombach derived from considerations more complex than his exchange with Burkart implies. Slightly more than a month after their discussion, Konrad Kaletsch reported to Flick that Hanneken, together with the chief of the German civil administration in Lorraine, had devised an alternative scheme for the incorporation of the steel plants of occupied Lorraine into the Reich in an "economically reasonable manner."[38] In contrast to the Foreign Office and Justice Ministry, which argued in favor of taking over only those plants expropriated from German owners in 1919, Hanneken argued that the established concerns of the German steel industry should be closed out of the expropriations altogether and that the assets be offered to "individuals" who agreed to follow through with the reconstruction programs required to revive production. The notion appealed to many in the Reich economics bureaucracy, especially those of an anti–big business bent who saw an opportunity to break up concentrations of economic power. One cannot but marvel at the sheer folly of such a plan in the light of Germany's war priorities; in the interest of social nicety, one suspects, Kaletsch generously assumed in his report to Flick that it was a mistake. Surely, he pointed out, Hanneken must have grasped that a redevelopment program would be inconceivable without the deep financial resources and technical capabilities of the large concerns. Nonetheless, it appeared that some time would pass before the authorities arrived at any firm decision on how best to deal with the new economic realities in Lorraine. As to the question of payment, Kaletsch drew

Flick's attention to the Finance Ministry's insistence that German concerns pay something approximating a market value for sequestered assets. Were rebated prices offered, the ministry expected to make up the difference in additional taxes.

On the same day Kaletsch submitted his report, 2 October, Flick finally brought forth a formal memorandum to Poensgen openly naming Rombach and Homecourt as his acquisition targets.[39] In justification, he argued that the Flick concern had patriotically defended the Kattowitz and Laura steel-works in Silesia against what he deemed a Polish "politics of thievery," surrendering them only reluctantly in 1936. Despite the circumstances of the current German acquisition program in Lorraine, it is doubtful that Flick grasped the irony in his claim. Following the German invasion in 1939, the Nazi government had promised the works in Poland to other interested parties, and Flick viewed an acquisition of Rombach and its mines as just compensation for his loss of some 7 million tons of hard coal and the high-value finishing operations of the Silesian steelworks. This argument does not appear in Flick's prior treatments on the topic; in fact, his deputy, Burkart, went out of his way in his dealings with Hanneken to downplay the relevance of prospects in Silesia for the Flick concern, perhaps fearing that the authorities would be tempted to offer Flick assets there that he really did not want. Why Flick assumed such arguments would resonate more strongly with Poensgen is unclear. Flick's other points were by now familiar. He claimed that the Reich government owed him a substantial concession on account of Harpen having turned over a sizable proportion of its surplus coal mines to the Reichswerke on behalf of the entire steel industry. Although he had received shares in East Elbian soft-coal operations as compensation, the uncertain coke supply situation in the Lorraine steel mills and his own surplus underscored the logic of giving him Rombach. Moreover, Flick proposed maintaining the partnership between Rombach and the nearby Homecourt plant, because their ore fields adjoined one another and because both had belonged ultimately to the French firm of Laurent, which had operated them throughout the interwar period. Important administrative and technical links between the firms had developed, particularly in their distribution and marketing mechanisms, and their continued affiliation seemed sensible. Most importantly, perhaps, to a rival industrialist like Poensgen, Flick pointed out that as a proportion of those French works to be distributed by the Reich, the total capacity of the two plants did not exceed Flick's total prewar share of the steel industry.

Only five days later, Flick dispatched a missive to Hanneken. By now, Flick had grown more adept at casting his appeals in terms he thought agreeable to the different parties involved. Referring to their earlier conversations of 9 and 24 September, Flick provided Hanneken with a carbon copy of his letter to Poensgen and drew his attention to the issues of the coke supply and the labor force, the latter of which had not figured in the letter.[40] Flick cited the supply of coking coal as the factor most hampering the resumption of steel production in Lorraine and reemphasized the surplus capacity of his concern in that respect. Apparently, Hanneken had earlier complained that supplying Rombach with coke as a component of Flick's larger concern would do nothing to alleviate the general shortage of coking coal available to the rest of the industry. Flick now replied that he had consulted with his staff on the matter and determined that with a modest supplemental allocation of labor and equipment from the authorities, his concern could match the supply requirements of the dependent steelworks—approximately 1 million tons annually—while supplying Rombach as well, which suggests that Flick had been effectively concealing from the authorities the true surplus capacities of his concern, most likely to avoid providing a pretext for a further surrender of resources to the Reichswerke. Flick did not elaborate on how he would wring such remarkable efficiencies from his operations. He also drew attention to the personnel question, which had figured only marginally in consultations up to this point. He pointed out that his concern had a large number of staff who had been active in the minette region in the recent past and whom the concern could make available to Rombach. The staff would relocate to Lorraine as well, obviously an advantage to a regime concerned with integrating the region more solidly into the Reich from a social perspective.

In his approach to Hanneken, Flick also referenced the fact that certain relevant official agencies apparently favored the distribution of assets only to firms owned by individuals and for which only individuals assumed full liability, a clear reference to preferences already attributed to Hanneken and Bürckel by Kaletsch. Rather disingenuously Flick argued that since the establishment of the Kommanditgesellschaft in 1937 he alone bore complete responsibility for the entire concern.[41] Vested therein was complete ownership of Mittelstahl and an indirect 85 percent control over Maxhütte, which was bound tightly in partnership to Mittelstahl and through which he further controlled Harpen and Essener. Through these byzantine arrangements Flick made a bizarre case for himself as a prime example of the stalwart, independent entrepreneur so dear to the ideological sensibilities of some Nazis. While adhering to the letter of Hanneken's proposal, which does not appear to have been advanced with much in the way of supporting ideological arguments or principled claims, Flick's argument certainly ran counter to its spirit. It seems safe to assume that Nazi emphasis on individual entrepreneurship as the bulwark of the German economy did not embrace examples of such scale and scope as Flick.

Flick also attempted in his letter to Hanneken to close out the Silesian option once and for all. He requested clarification from Hanneken about the contents of a letter of 5 August from Economics Minister Walther Funk to the director of the Haupttreuhandstelle Ost (the main trustee office for the eastern territories) regarding possible joint administration of expropriated works in both the occupied East and West. Funk had stated that the Flick concern was to be considered in the distribution of assets by virtue of its prior operations in the area. Flick now argued that consideration of his concern in the case of the Kattowitz/Laura works was no longer relevant, as the coal pits on which the plants were based had been reserved for other purposes and because the Bismarckhütte, the only smelting facility in Upper Silesia, had been given to a concern with no prior experience in the region. As a practical undertaking Kattowitz/Laura had been gutted, its prime coal deposits and chief processing outlets separated from the parent organization. In such a state it could not possibly serve as a substitute for Rombach.

In a strongly worded conclusion, Flick made clear to Hanneken that with the loss of his concern's Silesian holdings, he had no desire to be closed out of possibilities for expansion in the West on the basis of vague and inadequate allusions to eastern properties. "I wish to make clear on behalf of my group that our western claims should have precedence and that I make absolutely no claims for my group in the east, in case the latter is taken into account in a consideration of western claims or compensated with them."[42] He retained no interest in reacquiring those assets in Silesia that he had earlier lost, a possibility tentatively advanced by the trustee office for the eastern territories to offset an unfavorable distribution of spoils in the West. His concern had a strong moral claim to Rombach, he reiterated, a point recognized by virtually every relevant official party. The deceptive thrust to this line of argumentation becomes apparent when one considers Flick's aggressive attempts to acquire Rombach through purely practical arguments.

By 1 November 1940, Flick apparently felt that sufficient ground-work had been laid to make a formal appeal to Hermann Göring for the Rombach steelworks.[43] Preceded by a generous personal note and in reference to an earlier exchange at which Göring apparently promised to consider the needs of the Flick concern second only to those of the Reichswerke, Flick made use of his full panoply of open justifications: the loss in 1936 of his Upper Silesian operations; his surrender of large ore deposits to the Reichswerke in 1937–38 and of substantial hard-coal deposits in 1939; his concern's ability to assign experienced technical personnel and managers to operations in Lorraine; the capacity of his firm to supply an operation as large as Rombach with coking coal and provide the open market with a further million tons per year; and finally, the stated wish of the economics minister to handle expropriation issues pertaining to the West and East on a collective basis, which implied a recognition of Flick's "moral claim" to Rombach as a result of the loss of his production in Silesia, but without entertaining the possibility of alternative compensation there. Somewhat improbably, Flick indicated that no objections had issued from official circles, a point that appears to gloss over Hanneken's voiced unease.[44] The sources offer no indication whether Flick's specific arguments swayed Göring, in whom was vested final authority for the decision and for whom personal interactions were quite important. That Hanneken was thought to have influence in the matter is suggested by the Flick concern's overtures to him and the stature of his position within the economics bureaucracy. However, in the end it was Göring who awarded the Rombach properties to Flick.

In postwar testimony, Hanneken argued that he concurred with the decision to award the Rombach works to Flick to prevent the further expansion of the Reichswerke and VSt, which bid concurrently along with Flick and Röchling for control. Hanneken also cited "technical grounds" for favoring Flick, presumably meaning his ability to fuel the Rombach blast furnaces with coking coal from Harpen. Of course, in the same postwar statement, Hanneken acknowledged that ultimate authority to appoint trustees lay with Walther Funk and Göring, and that the latter had reached a final decision as to Rombach "on or shortly after" 10 January 1941.[45] Although offering no specifics, Hanneken apparently believed that Flick had somehow exercised undue personal influence on that occasion to promote his claim for Rombach, perhaps while Göring was under the influence of alcohol. That Hanneken was skeptical about the suitability of awarding the plant to Flick is clear from his interactions with concern officials prior to that point. Göring's decision to award the plant to Flick proved controversial in industrial circles as well and brought forth unusually blunt and strident invective from Hermann Röchling. Given his activities on behalf of the regime to that point, Röchling could fairly claim that his commitment to the National Socialist program, broadly construed, uniquely qualified him to benefit from its largesse. In a heated letter to Hanneken, Röchling charged that Göring's apportionment scheme slighted the Saar works undeservedly and that his own investment in low-grade ores and the production of synthetic fuels warranted more consideration in the distribution.[46] However, Röchling reserved his greatest ire for Flick, deriding him as a portfolio-builder without substantive experience or interest in actual operations and thus unfit for the sort of applied management required in Lorraine—not a true industrialist, in other words, but a speculator. Most damningly, Röchling argued that in avoiding any form of financial or political risk on behalf of the nation, and in not lining up against the Ruhr barons during the founding of the Reichswerke, Flick was politically unfit to receive a prize like Rombach. If the regime went ahead with its decision, Röchling wrote, he would consider it a personal insult. The evidence does not indicate whether Röchling's letter had an effect on Hanneken or Göring, to say nothing of Flick, assuming that he was made aware of its contents. However, the controversy quickly died out. Göring was not to be deterred. Röchling's complaint had no discern-

able effect on his future dealings with Flick as supervisor of the steel industry in the occupied West.[47]

Hanneken confirmed Göring's decision in a memorandum on 31
January 1941 distributed to the major steel industrialists by Reichert.
The directive appointed Flick to take over and manage the Rombach and
Machen works as trustee with the option of purchasing the works outright
upon conclusion of a peace "unless conditions are changed by circumstances."[48] As Hanneken put it in postwar testimony, neither the regime
nor the industrial community doubted that the trustees would be permitted to gain ownership over the plants after the war, although that codi-
cil did not emerge contractually until protracted negotiations had taken
place. An official in the office of the civil administrator for Lorraine for-
malized Flick's trusteeship over Rombach on 20 February 1941, confirm-
ing the transfer of control on Göring's authority as elaborated in a decree
of the economics minister.[49] The letter acknowledged that with the eventual conclusion of a final peace treaty between Germany and France, wartime trusteeship over the works would become full legal ownership. That
assurance notwithstanding, numerous appointees approached Hanneken
about the possibility of outright purchase during the war. When asked why
the regime opted not to dispense with the cumbersome legal and administrative machinery of the trustee system, Hanneken replied evasively after
the war that he had not considered wartime redistribution prudent.[50] With
time, the difficulties inherent in the trustee arrangement as conceived at
the outset led to friction between the economic bureaucracy and the trustees, difficulties that could have been avoided had ownership arrangements
been settled in 1941.

The regulatory framework drawn up by the office of the civil administrator situated the trustees within the arrangements made in the early
months of the occupation to manage the works on an emergency basis.
While removing immediate responsibility for the works from the pleni-
potentiaries for the iron and steel industry in Lorraine and Luxemburg,
Röchling and Steinbrinck, it left both of them in place to supervise the
trustees and represent their interests within the economy at large. It further
stipulated that the Economic Group Iron and Steel assume joint represen-
tation of the works at the level of national-interest groups, a configuration

that contributed to the blurring of lines separating private and public lines of economic oversight. The order did not alter the system of administration over those ore mines previously tied to smelting plants. Those were left under the overall administration of the plenipotentiary for mining in the occupied West, which ensured that the regime retained a measure of control over the lifeblood of the steelworks.[51] As should be apparent, the system superimposed one set of authorities over a prior set without clarifying in any material way the distinct mandate and limitations of each.

However, none of these complications was immediately troubling to the industrialists, who happily assumed control over their new plants. Flick in particular moved quickly to establish his presence and restart production. On 1 March 1941 Flick dispatched a letter to Bürckel assigning him responsibility for overseeing the implementation of the trustee agreements and announcing the formation of a new firm, Rombacher Hüttenwerke GmbH, with an initial capitalization of RM 500,000. Flick chose to establish the headquarters of the new company not in Rombach but in Saarbrücken, citing the ongoing force of formal French law in Lorraine and promising to transfer the headquarters as soon as the authorities applied German law there. The existing provisions of the German coal syndicate of which Flick was a member stipulated that the different firms in a supply chain be wholly owned; thus, Harpener Bergwerke assumed a 51 percent controlling stake in the new company, which supposedly assured Rombach a supply of coking coal, while the remaining 49 percent was assumed by Maxhütte. Flick decided to mingle the two firms because their production programs were similar and the overlap in the areas of their respective markets made for possible efficiencies in that respect.[52] The substantial minority stake by Maxhütte also provided for the transfer of numerous key personnel from the latter to Rombach, most notably General Director Karl Raabe, a talented manager who took overall charge of the plant's operations.[53] Official transfer of control was enshrined in a contract that marked an end to Röchling's interim administration of the plant and that he was made to sign, no doubt to his chagrin.[54] Flick thereby assumed formal control of the Rombach steelworks on 1 March 1941.

That the trusteeship was intended by the authorities to imply final ownership after the war could not have been in doubt, as numerous allusions to such an outcome by senior officials in the months leading up to the transfer attest. Indeed, it is safe to assume that only the possibility of securing final ownership offered the wartime trustees sufficient motive to maintain and operate the plants in as efficient a manner as possible, to say nothing of providing the substantial investments required to modernize them. Open-ended management arrangements would have left the Lorraine steel industry to deteriorate gradually and compromised the potential for heightened war output.

Consistent with that insight, subsequent negotiations between the Flick concern and the economic authorities centered on the specific parameters of the trustee agreement. Flick sought to define more tightly the contractual right to purchase the plants outright or under more favorable terms with the conclusion of a peace treaty. He also sought to alter the existing agreement to permit him to operate Rombach less as a trustee than as an entrepreneur. The differences are noteworthy and derive chiefly from the assessment of risk in each case. A trustee nominally assumes responsibility for an asset on behalf of another party, which mitigates both the risks inherent in negative economic outcomes and the incentive to investing more than warranted by the lesser returns generally permitted a trustee; an entrepreneur, in contrast, assumes either full risk or a much higher risk for the economic outcome and stands to reap the full benefits from his investment. The Nazi regime sought to retain some prerogative over the final disposition of the plants in question to ensure that they were operated properly, or merely to retain some presence in the decision-making of the industrialists in question. Understandably, Flick clearly sought an arrangement that protected his potential investments and his freedom to dispose of the asset as he saw fit. His desire to secure full control reflected how little financial risk he saw in his acquisition, a sign of the optimism with which he thought the plant could be profitably run.

As the economic authorities insisted that the eventual purchase price of the plants approximate their market value, a formal appraisal of their facilities and production potential played a key role in determining the character of the trustee arrangement and the desirability of the plants to the German industrial community. Too high an assessed value made them unappealing as investments in the postwar steel market, since demand for steel would undoubtedly contract; too low a value stood to distort the structure of the steel industry and the distributional relationships among the leading producers. The Economics Ministry appointed a commission headed by Hugo Klein, director and chairman of the board of the Siegener Hütte, on 21 February 1941 to survey the plants throughout the occupied western territories and estimate their value. Final deliberations took place in late April. The commission submitted a twenty-one-page report detailing the methodology whereby it arrived at its estimate, drafts of the leasing contracts, and a full description of the plants in question.[55] Following a relatively straightforward system of multiplying the yearly output of the plants by the estimated cost per ton of steel produced, the commission valued Rombach at RM 23.4 million, a figure that would be the object of some dispute in subsequent negotiations.

Uncertainty regarding the final disposition of the plants after the conclusion of a peace treaty with France complicated the implementation of trusteeships. Hans Hahl, a minor industrialist responsible for overseeing several of the smaller French steel firms, circulated a memorandum in May 1941 that brought a number of the most pressing issues to the fore.[56] Early drafts of the trustee contract[57] apparently lacked an explicit assurance that the trustees would have the option of purchasing the plants outright, a crucial earlier stipulation by Göring that led to the rush by industrialists for holdings in the West.[58] Rejecting earlier arrangements already in force in Upper Silesia, whereby the trustee office for the eastern territories offered industrialists control over plants without an option to purchase, Hahl's circular suggested that the final contract either include a "right of preemption and/or title for option," or be drawn up expressly as a contract of sale.

Prospective trustees developed a more concentrated list of contractual points at a meeting on 27 May 1941 attended by Flick's deputy, Burkart, in preparation for a conference with a senior economics official in the Gau administration in Saarbrücken scheduled for early June. Expressing dismay that the draft contract offered by the authorities in no way met the expectations raised by the Economics Ministry in January, the industrialists urged firstly that a "workable preliminary contract of sale" be developed, consistent with precedents already established by Mannesmann in Luxemburg or by IG Farben in its acquisition of the Luxemburg firm of

Air-Liquide. Should the stronger claim not be possible, the authorities should at the very least respect the "right of option" to later purchase cited earlier by the ministry. They conceded as acceptable the possibility that a second, separate agreement could guarantee that same option.[59]

Underlying the seemingly superficial issue of optioned purchasing was the more contentious one of rents. Under the terms of the trustee agreement, firms would pay the Reich government a certain annual amount of rent per ton of pig iron or steel produced in the leased plants, a sum that they insisted should count against the eventual purchase price established by the Klein Commission. Net profits, the industrialists argued, should be calculated only after calculated depreciation of key assets and after suitable provision had been made for taxes and remuneration. Depreciation of the assets obviously had to figure in any trustee agreement with an option to purchase, but the industrialists doubted that depreciations could figure in a pure lease agreement of the sort put forth in the original draft: "For this reason alone it must be attempted to establish the possibility of purchase at a later date . . . and retroactive from 1 March 1941, in order to secure sufficient tax reductions in later negotiations with the revenue office."[60]

The conference to which the above meeting of representatives had been preliminary took place on 6 June 1941.[61] Flick himself, accompanied by Burkart and Raabe (who had by that point assumed the directorship of the Rombach works), met with a senior economic official in Bürckel's office of the civil administrator. Burkart first stumped the official with the rather simple question of whether any future contract should be concluded with the Friedrich Flick KG or with the corporation established to manage the works, Rombacher Hüttenwerke GmbH. The official had no answer. However, he readily agreed to the idea that a full option to later purchase, contingent on the establishment of peacetime condition, should be explicitly included in the preamble to the trustee agreement.

In brief, Flick and his subordinates advanced a list of negotiation points to be considered by the authorities in a final contract. Most important was a clear formulation of the purchase option mentioned in the letter of the Economics Ministry on 31 January 1941. Most of the other points derived in some manner from the first. Flick demanded that the government fix contractually the value of the plants as determined by the Klein

Commission as the price to be paid for later purchase and sought a promise that trustee firms would not be liable for losses in the event that they failed to attain a given percentage of the output capacity defined in the contract. He also wanted the contract to stipulate that the trustee firm should receive control of adjacent facilities and mining pits; the omission from the trustee contract of any mention of depreciation to avoid complications with the tax authorities; a counting of the 90 pfennig tax per ton of crude iron or steel against the contractually established purchase price of the plants; and finally, a removal of the obligation to secure the approval of the civil administrator for Lorraine for all major investments, to be replaced by an obligation merely to report such investments, subject to his right of intervention.[62] The final stipulation would do much to liberate Flick from the most direct and intrusive form of state control over his operations in Lorraine.

Although those present at the conference on 6 June discussed the issue of depreciation, fuller clarification of the topic did not emerge until Dr. Koob, chief of the economic office of the civil administrator, wrote a letter to both Flick and the Rombach works on 30 July addressing their concerns.[63] Koob had conferred with the Economics Ministry on 14 July, which held that a formal and contractual option to purchase was "out of the question," insisting instead that the decree of 31 January, which had named the trustees and cited a purchase option, constituted guarantee enough. Although the ministry deemed that no alteration of the draft contract itself was necessary, it requested that a copy of the decree be affixed to the final contract as an addendum.

As for the contractual fixing of a purchase price for a later date based on the assessment of the Klein Commission, the ministry insisted that basic economics dictated against establishing in 1941 a price to be paid at an indeterminate future date, which could well be years in advance.[64] The regime's position on this point was an eminently reasonable one. Much could happen in the intervening time to enhance or degrade the value of the assets, not the least of which would be substantial investment by trustee firms to boost their competitiveness. However, it also meant that the trustee had a strong interest in ensuring that investment would not actually work against his interests in the purchasing process later by increasingly the value of the plant, or inversely by burdening him with excess capacity in a much-contracted postwar market. Thus, the anticipated postwar level of demand for steel could powerfully influence the appeal of the plants to industrialists whose chief concern in 1941 was fulfillment of massive armaments contracts. The ministry was prepared at this point to offer no more than an essentially good-faith guarantee: "[T]here is no need to fear that receiving plants, should they make substantial investments . . . would have to pay for these investments a second time." The ministry went on to encourage Flick, "in view of the advanced date," to formulate his final comments as quickly as possible and fix a date for the signing of the final contract. It also insisted that the draft put forth by the Klein Commission, in light of its being composed of "disinterested specialists and government officials," serve as the basis for the final contract.

In essence, the Reich government sought to have private industrialists assume control of the plants and invest the necessary capital and resources to improve and run them without any binding, enforceable guarantee that they could eventually purchase the installations at a price that reflected the quality of their stewardship. There should be little wonder that Flick reacted with skepticism. At this point, one must wonder whether Flick understood that the same ruthless opportunism that had created such remarkable opportunities to enrich himself stood at odds with the precepts of a lawful, contractually bound society in which he, as a businessman, had a stake. If he did, his manifest desire to profit from the situation gave no hint of it.

Flick could derive some confidence that he would eventually gain control of the Rombach works on favorable terms from developments in the eastern theater of war, where a drive for acquisition of sequestered works had assumed an importance secondary to the need to clarify future ownership rights, in no small part as a result of the private industry having already confronted similar issues in the West. Göring took steps to address those concerns almost immediately after the German invasion, when he declared his intention to reprivatize state assets at the end of the war. The Nazi regime would be guided by the principle that only on "the proven foundation of (state-guided) private enterprise" could an efficient economy be organized. The regime would uphold a statist approach in the East only to maintain control over those elements crucial to the war economy for as long as was necessary. Private enterprise would eventually govern the development of the German economy, provided it did not stray from Nazi expectations.[65] Obviously, the latter provision left much potential room for official abuse and ample grounds for almost any kind of intervention. Nonetheless, Flick's chief deputy for steel issues, Burkart, confirmed his faith in the regime's intentions toward private industry in a memorandum of August 1941 detailing a conversation he had held with an official of the Four-Year Plan organization. According to the official, Göring had repeatedly declared his desire to reprivatize state industrial holdings, possibly including the Reichswerke, at the conclusion of hostilities. Of special importance was the fact that Hitler appeared to agree entirely with Göring that a postwar decrease in state involvement in the economy was desirable.[66] Based on his willingness to believe such intelligence, Flick could have confidence that even limited ownership stakes had the potential to become more substantial later on.

The final contract of 15 December 1942 reflected the compromises reached in the course of the negotiations. It stipulated that Flick was to pay 90 pfennigs for every ton of crude iron and crude steel produced, as well as interest on the assessed value of the plant, which was set at RM 26.3 million.[67] The interest was calculated on the basis of standard guidelines governing prices and costs for public contracts. The contract allowed for a reduction in interest payments against the value of the plant in the event of a failure to attain the rate of production estimated by the Klein Commission. To guard against attempts to use the asset as an insured repository for excess capital as well as to regulate the financing of industrial activities, investments exceeding RM 500,000 in value required the consent of the civil administrator in Lorraine. Bürckel, therefore, retained an oversight role in the firm's operations. Quite generously, failure to purchase the plant upon termination of the contract entitled Flick to reimbursement of approved investments. The contract also appointed an authority for binding arbitration of contractual disputes between the Flick concern and the Reich government.

Flaws in the terms of the contract provided leverage through which Flick later attempted a revision designed to solidify his position as the outright owner of Rombach. At a conference with Reich officials held at the headquarters of the Reichswerke on 19 January 1943, Kaletsch pointed out that in establishing a series of royalties and levies to be set against an inde-terminate future purchase price, the contract made it almost impossible for Rombach to amortize its tax load for the duration of the contract.[68] Such an arrangement also introduced an anomalous element into the pub-lic finances of the civil administration of Lorraine, which had apparently counted the royalties paid on output and interest on the assessed value as incoming revenue instead of placing them in a holding account against later purchase of the plants. That this procedure was inappropriate appar-ently came as "quite a shock" to the budgetary manager of the civil admin-istration, who had apparently not been fully apprised of the terms of the contract. Two of the officials present agreed with Kaletsch that the prevail-ing arrangement had serious flaws and supported his pressing for clarifica-tion of the end state of the trusteeship.

In a discussion only a day later with officials from the Finance and Economics Ministries and the Reichswerke, Kaletsch again reiterated the Flick concern's "fundamental objections" to the draft contract of 15 December 1942. He had refined his arguments to emphasize the fact that the contract would not give Rombach the ability to write off amortizations and keep accurate financial records. In that way, the contract could not be said to reflect Göring's original rationale that only the still-undeter-mined political status of relations with France postponed conveyance of the works to the trustees. Kaletsch emphasized that the Flick concern had from the outset considered itself the entrepreneur of Rombach, investing "considerable sums" and transferring its best personnel to operate it. He demanded that the concern be permitted amortizations for the old plant (Altanlagen) in order to carry out the capital improvements required to make it competitive. Were they not permitted, Kaletsch argued, Rombach's profit statements would not reflect its actual financial condition, which could complicate the calculation of a fair purchase price later on. Necessary investments would be out of the question were Flick compelled to operate the plant as a pure lessee.[69]

To be fair, it seems that Kaletsch interpreted the likely outcome of the trustee contract in unduly negative terms. However, his objections had merit and the reply of the senior Finance Ministry official present was overly categorical: no sale would be considered at the present, indeed chiefly because Göring himself was opposed, whatever his original intention may have been. Furthermore, because the Flick concern did not actually own the works, Flick and the other trustees would not be permitted to write off amortizations on properties that did not formally belong to them. Finally, contradicting directly Kaletsch's negative portrayal of its terms, the official expressed bewilderment that Flick could interpret anything in the contract to suggest that investments would necessarily result in loss were they not differently booked.

In response, Kaletsch tried another tack. He argued that according to the contract, investment and improvement would be refunded only to the extent that an inventory remained on the plant's books. Improvements not appearing as inventory could be neither refunded nor subsequently written off as amortizations for tax purposes. To this the Finance Ministry officials reacted more favorably, agreeing that the contract should include a clause refunding all investments and improvements regardless of whether they appear on the balance sheet. In a larger sense, Kaletsch had succeeded in painting a compelling picture of the trustee contract's shortcomings and in demonstrating the virtues of, if not outright ownership, an arrangement with bookkeeping and tax advantages comparable to those of ownership. As if to drive home the fact that the matter was frustrating to all parties, not just the industrialists, two of the three Finance officials agreed that the plants should be sold to the trustees as quickly as possible, expressing dissatisfaction with the accounting ambiguities of the contracts.[70]

The most interesting result of the conference was the reaction of one of the Finance Ministry officials to the entire project at hand. The official had been tasked with overseeing the liquidation of German assets in Lorraine during negotiations over the Versailles Treaty in 1919 and administering the compensation paid out to Germany for the plants. The prices paid by the French on that occasion, he held, were "so low as to be scandalous." Surprisingly, however, he argued that in the present case, the prices established by the Klein Commission were even lower than those allowed by the French, an assertion not verifiable with the available evidence. In a remarkable attack of conscience, the official indicated that in his current role as one of the custodians of enemy property, he could not justify doing for another party what he had condemned on the part of the French, especially as he had written books on the subject. To his objections, Kaletsch weakly retorted that the French had performed almost nothing beyond the barest maintenance between 1918 and 1940, leaving the plants in very poor condition.

In the end the official's objections came to nothing. Final discussions over the terms of the contract resulted in an outcome, according to Kaletsch, "as we wished as far as we are concerned."[71] The Reich government acceded to virtually all of the Flick concern's proposed contractual revisions and proceeded with the trusteeship on terms agreeable to the firm, meaning terms that minimized the risk incurred in the operation of the plants and virtually guaranteed the option to purchase later on advantageous terms. Sale of the installations to the trustees would take place on the basis of those conditions in which the plants were found on 1 March 1941.[72] The civil administration in Lorraine would refund the wartime taxes paid on output and count them against the depreciation caused by operation of the installations in the service of the Reich. To deal with the possibility that a trustee would not acquire the plant and have to sacrifice investments and amortizations made during his tenure, the revised contract provided for a "special balance sheet" that reflected the investments and their amortization for subsequent tax purposes.[73] In essence, this provided for two separate accounts and allowed the trustee to operate the property as his own, take advantage of advantageous tax provisions in Lorraine that encouraged investments in capital, and all the while retain the profits from those investments (subject to appropriate taxation) in the event that sale did not materialize. Disputes over the validity and execution of the contractual terms would be referred to an arbitration panel seated in Saarbrücken.[74] The contract thus balanced entrepreneurial incentives for wartime production with the preference of the Reich government to set the ultimate question of ownership aside for the duration of the conflict.[75]

The potential for the Flick concern in a successful acquisition of the Rombach steelworks cannot be overstated. In an official report of 29 May 1941 on the place of the Reichswerke within the German steel industry, the Flick concern occupied the fourth position overall with a production total of some 1.82 million tons of pig iron, or some 5.9 percent of the total.[76] In that section of the report forecasting future iron and steel production in the Greater German Reich, including Lorraine, the total estimated output was 40.18 million tons, of which the Flick concern, including Rombach, accounted for 2.49 million tons, or some 6.2 percent of the total and a noteworthy increase within the overall production of the industry. Internal calculations by the Flick concern generated similar results. Tonnage capacity in the Rombach plant was estimated at 820,000 tons, assuming a constant rate of maximum production without further development of the installation.[77] The addition of Rombach to the Flick concern thus brought the potential total of his steel operations from 8.86 to 9.35 percent of total German steel production. As Flick soon learned, however, the complications of wartime expansion would lead to an enormous gap between potential and reality.

Friedrich Flick testifies during his postwar trial in 1947.

U.S. National Archives and Records Administration

Odilo Burkhart testifies at Nuremburg. Burkhart was one of Flick's closest associates and agents in several of the firms within the Flick concern, as well as Flick's chief deputy for iron, steel, and coal-related matters.

Josef Bürckel (2nd from left), Chef der Zivilverwaltung in Lothringen, in conference with Adolf Hitler, accompanied by Wilhelm Frick (left) and Rudolf Hess (2nd from right). *U.S. National Archives and Records Administration*

Otto Steinbrinck
U.S. National Archives and Records Administration

Friedrich Flick
U.S. National Archives and Records Administration

Odilo Burkart
U.S. National Archives and Records Administration

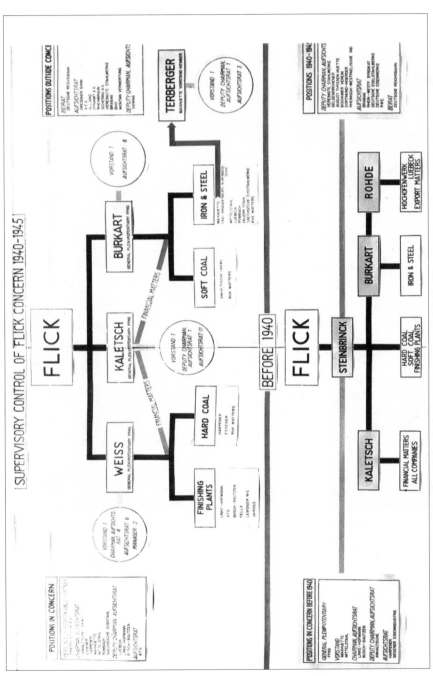

Chart Depicting the Corporate Structure of the Flick Concern during World War II.

U.S. National Archives and Records Administration

Steel Production Hall, Rombach Steelworks
Bayerisches Wirtschaftsarchiv, F70/539

CHAPTER 5

THE SIGNIFICANCE OF LORRAINE FOR THE GERMAN STEEL INDUSTRY AND THE FLICK CONCERN'S ADMINISTRATION OF THE ROMBACH WORKS, 1941-1944

The Flick concern's administration of the Rombach steelworks from 1941 to late 1944 was beset from the start by complications that hindered full realization of its potential. Despite a lengthy and expensive campaign to improve the plant under the terms of his trusteeship, Flick never succeeded in overcoming the difficulties in supplying it adequately with coking coal or achieving the low *Selbstkosten* that had in part served to justify the acquisition. Although Flick's trusteeship enjoyed some success in manufacturing munitions and sponsoring French firms doing the same through a German government program set up for that purpose, it fell victim to the same basic problems that plagued the German steel industry generally throughout this period. Administrative problems associated with managing a major industrial operation under the Nazi regime, supply and distribution issues (especially of coking coal), labor difficulties, and the poor state of the works themselves all stood in the way of full utilization.

The Flick concern was not the only German firm to have difficulty with its new acquisition. The German steel industry at large was in an uncertain state as the trustees appointed by Göring took over the plants in Lorraine in 1941. As detailed earlier, heavy reliance on imports of iron in the interwar period had evoked concerns among Nazi officials about the ability of the industry to sustain the war effort. The exploitation of the ore mines and steel plants of newly conquered territories was thought to address that vulnerability and provide ready access to inexpensive productive capacity. In the event, fears about the ore basis of German steel production proved groundless. Imports from Germany's chief foreign supplier, Sweden, continued reliably throughout the most intense years of the war, contrary to the baleful predictions of industrialists and officials alike.[1]

The only noteworthy exceptions were the months following the outbreak of war in 1939 and the final months of 1944 and early 1945. The outbreak of war temporarily interrupted almost all supplies of ore from abroad except those from Sweden, reducing Germany's supplies in a matter of weeks by nearly a third.[2] Almost as quickly, however, Germany's success in the western campaign against France promised to alleviate the shortfall with the rich minette of eastern France, thus lessening the overall proportion of imported ores in German production. Therefore, the war both necessitated and facilitated a broadening of the raw materials base of the German steel industry, with the ore produced in the minette basin accounting for more than half of the total from the sources controlled by the Nazi regime.[3] The conquest of Lorraine and incorporation of its ore mines, therefore, fulfilled the expectations of planners and industry both that the German war effort would not be vulnerable in that critical respect.

With the mines of eastern France under German control and an ongoing supply of Swedish ore, domestic production of steel continued throughout the war at high levels. Output in 1943, for example, was 1.5 times greater than the average between 1936 and 1938, even in the face of aggressive Allied bombing.[4] Nevertheless, armaments producers consistently lacked enough steel to fulfill the demands of the services, at times to an extent alarming to economic planners.[5] In particular, demand for the high-quality finished steel manufactured from high-grade ore escalated continually between 1939 and 1945.[6] To some extent one can attribute shortfalls in supply to the high level of demand. But other factors also limiting an increase in production included an inefficient use of blast-furnace capacity, shortages of suitable coking coal, and a consistent inability to retain a reliable labor force in the face of wartime mobilization and dislocation.[7] The lattermost factor was a particularly sore point for industrialists like Flick, who pointed out after the war that an "increase in production depended on a sufficient quality of minette, that is, ore from Lorraine, and this again depended on having sufficient labor."[8]

The first two factors hindering the desired increase in steel production—inefficient use of blast-furnace capacity and a shortage of coke—resulted to a considerable extent from the chronically overtaxed and poorly organized transportation system, the Achilles' heel of the entire German war economy. In early 1940 Göring cited a solution to the transportation problem as one of the most urgent economic priorities facing Germany and went so far as to contemplate the appointment of a general plenipotentiary in the event that the Economics Ministry failed to solve it.[9] At no point before or during the war was German shipping fully adequate to the task of supplying the major German producers with the quantities of ore required to use fully their dormant blast-furnace capacity.[10] A deficient construction program and heavy losses during the war reduced the number of German ships available for these tasks, forcing the Swedish merchant fleet to make up the deficit. Likewise, the German rail network failed consistently to win the bureaucratic battles required to secure the locomotives, wagons, or trackage to cart the ore and coking coal to the steel plants.[11] Industrialists as well as transportation officials argued in vain for an ambitious production program to rectify these shortcomings, which would have involved greater allocations of material and capital to the construction of additional railroad equipment.[12]

Their pleas fell on deaf ears. Planners deemed the transportation systems of secondary importance to feeding the voracious appetite for steel of the Reichswerke Hermann Göring, which had, of course, been established to undercut or eliminate entirely Germany's dependence on foreign ores. The inefficiencies involved in processing low-grade domestic ore eventually compelled the Reichswerke itself to make extensive use of imported ores, a source of cynical amusement to partisans of private industry.[13] Management decisions out of touch with the financial constraints of the steel industry likewise did little to contribute to the greater good of the German war effort.[14] That Nazi Germany embarked on a project designed explicitly to provide for economic autarky without any clear appreciation of the requirements to achieve it underscores the almost complete dissonance between economic and strategic planning in Hitler's Germany.[15]

A similar unwillingness to engage in realistic planning characterized government initiatives under the Four-Year Plan to spur an increase of private steel production through the expansion of existing plants or construction of new ones in a host of venues. The War Economy Staff of the Wehrmacht High Command, among the few government agencies with an appreciation of what a war against the European powers demanded, estimated as early as November 1939 that the expansion of capacity then anticipated would require some 600,000 tons of iron and steel.[16] Assuming a time to completion of approximately two years, the new installations would have to operate thereafter at full capacity for a year and a half simply to replace the material invested. In a November 1939 conference with General Georg Thomas, head of the war economy staff, two leading steel industrialists emphasized the greater likely return on the substantial dormant capacity of already-existing plants. Better yet, they argued, would be to shut down less efficient operations temporarily and permit more modern facilities to make use of their technological advantages. This would free up scarce labor and investment resources, as well as provide a valuable impetus to further innovation and rationalization in the steel industry as a whole. The real issue was not capacity, but efficient usage, an argument that resonates strongly with contemporary economic theory. Were the regime to proceed otherwise, the industrialists argued, it risked an actual decline in iron and steel production over the medium term, especially in view of the precarious state of the transportation system.[17]

In view of these issues, already-existing plants in Lorraine represented a potential boon to the German steel industry as it struggled to meet wartime demand in 1940, a prospect that depended, in turn, on the efforts of the trustees who acquired them. Despite the nominally open-ended character of the trusteeship, Flick's intention was to manage the Rombach works as though they were a wholly owned component of his concern, no different than Mittelstahl, Maxhütte, or Harpen.[18] Consistent with his typical management approach, the plant was intended to function in as self-sustaining a fashion as possible, "to stand on its own feet and manage on its own," as one of Flick's chief deputies put it after the war.[19] As few could assume even in 1941 that steel mills in Lorraine would enjoy easy access to iron ore, coking coal, and labor under the circumstances of wartime, the resources and expertise of a major German concern could well determine whether Rombach would become a steady contributor to the German war effort. The first major hurdle to restoring Rombach was the supply of adequate coking coal, a clear problem in view of industry-wide shortages in 1941. Flick's claim that he could adequately supply the plant, made in the course of his lobbying campaign to win the trusteeship, was put to the test from the outset and ultimately shown to be empty. For a host of reasons Rombach did not enjoy a sufficient supply of coking coal even in the first months of Flick's management, to say nothing of the troubles encountered later. Average monthly supply until August 1941 amounted to only 89 percent of requirements, which led to production shortfalls at every step of production from raw steel to finished rolled goods.[20]

Flick initially appointed a senior official from his Maxhütte plant, Karl Raabe, to run Rombach while grooming his youngest son, Otto-Ernst, to assume control after a stint in the plant's administration. Otto-Ernst Flick, who eventually occupied the house of the Rombach general director in nearby Boussange, was only 23 years old when Göring conferred the trusteeship upon his father. On leaving school in 1935 he had received training in business management and joined Rombach in 1941, rising to business manager in the purchases and sales department only a year later, perhaps due to his talent but no doubt also by consequence of his father's position. In 1943 he took over the formal directorship of the Rombach works and assumed responsibilities broad for a man of his age and not unlike his father in the years before World War I, when the elder Flick joined the governing board of Menden & Schwerte as a young entrepreneur. Otto Flick's administration of Rombach was reputedly distinguished by its moderation; he was later described by an employee as enjoying constructive relations with the labor force, although the extent to which this can be true in a firm that eventually employed a large number of forced laborers is open to question. It is unclear from the evidence to what extent, if any, he trafficked with the workers under his control. He reportedly eschewed the Nazi salute (although he signed his official correspondence with the requisite "Heil Hitler") and insisted that his domestic staff converse in French, which he and his wife (the daughter, it should be pointed out, of the prior director) apparently spoke fluently.[21]

In seeking to bring Rombach up to the standard of the German steel industry and make it productive and profitable, the Flick concern faced significant obstacles beyond an inadequate supply of fuel for the blast furnaces. The poor physical condition of the works—which Hermann Röchling, who had formal responsibility for the plant before the trusteeship was awarded to Flick, described after the war as "very bad"—necessitated a massive investment program directed at virtually every aspect of their operation.[22] On a tour of Rombach in February 1941 led by Karl Raabe and a member of the German economic administration in Lorraine, senior Flick concern officials were informed that the plant was in dire need of some RM 40 million in renovations, a staggering sum when one recalls that the Klein Commission had estimated the value of the entire works at approximately RM 26 million.[23] Items requiring attention ranged from the peripheral, such as renovated barracks for the plant's labor force, to the indispensable, such as the massive rolling mills that turned out the finished steel.

Astonishingly, the evidence suggests that Flick had not reckoned with such an enormous potential renovation cost in his bid for the trustee-ship. After the war, Odilo Burkart, the Flick concern official responsible for steel production, described his discovery of the poor condition of the works and the scale of renovation required as "a real blow."[24] Flick him-self later estimated that the money expended in machine equipment alone came to RM 5–8 million, an amount that included, among other things, the relocation and installation of an entire rolling mill assembly from one of his other works in Germany. If anything, Flick's postwar estimate of the costs was most probably too low. According to the Maxhütte official tasked with assessing and reviving the works, the total sum eventually invested in new physical apparatus and other items amounted to RM 15–20 million.[25] How much Flick had anticipated investing in Rombach before assuming the trusteeship is unclear, but it seems unlikely that so experienced an industrialist as Flick would have made a decision to acquire a major steel plant without detailed forecasts of costs and returns based on a rigorous appraisal of the property, unless the value of the property was so low or the likely return on investment so high as to make the cost of renovations, however exorbitant, irrelevant.[26] It also seems unlikely that the poor state of the works can be attributed to the effects of the hasty French evacua-tion or the war itself. The reaction of Flick executives to the reconstruction expenses therefore leaves unanswered the question of whether the infor-mation about Rombach available to Flick in 1940 was accurate, and if so, why he chose to take on such a sizable burden in wartime. In any event, he averred after the war that he had sunk more into the plant in three and a half years than the previous French administration had in ten.[27] In light of what Flick executives encountered upon examination of their newly acquired asset, his claim rings true.

Flick immediately allocated substantial sums to the improvement of Rombach, which suggests transparently that he anticipated a worthwhile payoff over the long term. No matter what view one takes of his motives in acquiring Rombach, the renovation program he adopted makes sense only if he was laying the groundwork for permanent ownership. The most expensive parts of the renovation program addressed the physical infrastructure and therefore stood to enhance considerably the overall value and productivity of the works. In a memorandum in late November 1943, Otto-Ernst Flick wrote that "at the outset of our trusteeship we found a dilapidated and, in terms of its physical plant, badly operated work; as a result we strove to bring the plant up to the level demanded by current methods and guarantee that the most technical and economical results were achieved." He anticipated reconstruction of virtually every major system, beginning with the measures necessary to bring it up to the technological standards of German industry at large.[28]

Direct investment in an industrial operation under the regulatory conditions of the Nazi regime required a lengthy bureaucratic campaign and much patience on the part of the investor. The local administration constituted the first line of oversight. In his role as civil administrator in Lorraine, Bürckel reserved the right to approve any new construction or expansion of existing facilities in the iron and steel industry there. He also asserted the right of his administration to require the resumption of production in any facility dormant for longer than six months after 15 May 1941.[29] Guidelines obliged industrialists to apply for approval to allocate investment capital for any expansion of plant capacity greater than 15 percent, a process overseen in the case of most forms of steel by the civil administration and the Reich Office for Economic Improvement.[30] Application procedures were detailed and subject to review by the lengthy list of bureaucrats with a stake in the process. Finally, the Reich Office for Economic Improvement evaluated each application according to uniform guidelines designed to "safeguard the systematically planned expansion of the German steel industry."[31] The entire oversight process could take many months. Conformity to bureaucratic formula was of greater importance than the need to bring the plant back on line quickly, it seems.

During his trusteeship, Flick's efforts to improve Rombach had to comply with this frustratingly complex and time-consuming process. By the third month of 1942, his concern had submitted to the civil administration in Lorraine a detailed plan for "urgent new construction" costing more than RM 10.6 million to make possible renovations without which the plant could not function in its "intended manner," as a memorandum put it.[32] The plan left no doubt as to the poor initial condition of the works and addressed not superfluities but fundamental infrastructure. In some cases, this necessitated the purchase and installation of entirely new and expensive equipment to replace machinery more than thirty years old.[33] However, even a plan as basic as this met with skepticism from the authorities, who at times seemed less motivated by an urgency to reconstruct the Lorraine steel industry than were the industrialists running it. The cause, according to Flick, was the decision of the Reichswerke to undertake a massive investment program at around the same time and expand its operations beyond their already-distended point, which was thought to render heavy investments in capacity elsewhere unnecessary.[34] A further hindrance was ongoing talks between the Flick concern and the Economics Ministry concerning the specific manner whereby the Lorraine works should be permitted to finance renovations through adjusted depreciation accounting.[35] As discussed in the previous chapter, the issue of depreciation was a sore point in the negotiations between the trustees and the Reich government over the administration of the plants, and it is understandable that Flick had concerns over the manner in which his investment was accounted. Were he, through some unforeseeable happenstance, not to retain control over the plant after the conclusion of a peace treaty with France, failure to book his required improvements in an appropriate manner could cost him millions.

As the years of Flick's trusteeship wore on, the plant management progressed beyond restarting the works to a series of major and minor campaigns to bring them up to the industry standard. The most notable among these was a controversial and risky RM 5.56 million outlay in September 1943 for a new system to break, filter, and sinter raw iron ore, which was intended to extend the plant's operation more deeply into the vertical production process.[36] As late as 1944, with Germany's military fortunes sinking rapidly, the Flick concern paid more than RM 1.6 million for an extensive new furnace system.[37] But even these measures paled in comparison to a projected total outlay of RM 12.7 million for the calendar years 1944 and 1945. This was the largest expansion envisioned at a single stroke for any part of the Flick concern and a sizable proportion of the concern's total investment scheme.[38] That Flick would approve such an ambitious and expensive undertaking is surprising, given Germany's very poor strategic position at that late date in the war and the doubtful prospects for demand in a postwar steel market. It also raises the question of whether Flick was foolish enough in 1944 to suppose that in any plausible postwar environment he could reasonably expect to defend the asset-ownership arrangements he had won in 1940–41.

Infrastructure and production were not the only targets of Flick's investment. Measures required to keep the works running during the early renovation process consumed large amounts of capital that in more normal times would have been spread out over many years. A listing of pending investment programs as of August 1943 not subject to the oversight of the authorities, either because the programs were not large enough or because they did not involve issues requiring approval, included a number of minor expenditures ranging from initiatives for labor and administration to improved facilities for finishing refined goods and new processing facilities for armaments.[39] Viewed through these measures as well as those directed at infrastructure, it seems clear that Flick envisioned owning the works indefinitely and not merely extracting the greatest amount of profit from them in the shortest possible term. It also seems clear that, the official oversight process notwithstanding, the regime permitted Flick to operate the Rombach works in a manner similar to his plants in Germany proper. Flick certainly had to deal with conditions specific to doing business in the new territories of the Reich, most of which had to do with the ambiguous wartime status of Lorraine and the oversight authority of the civil administrator. Of course, one may attribute the entire institution of trusteeships to the anomalous conditions that obtained in Lorraine relative to those in Germany. The key point, however, is that those complications do not appear to have brought about any outcome not otherwise sought by the Flick concern. There is little to suggest that the plants in Lorraine were broadly understood to be different from those in the Altreich.

All the same, the fact that the Rombach works lay in Lorraine probably contributed most to what can only be called the failure of Flick's trusteeship, quite apart from the larger fate of the German war effort. Largely for reasons beyond its control, the concern failed to manage the plant in a manner that fully exploited the presumed advantages of steelworks in Lorraine, and Rombach turned out to be a poor acquisition for the Flick concern. Flick's original motive for acquiring control over a steelworks in the new territories lay partially with the exceptionally low cost of production in a region with direct access to abundant ore. However, he failed to weigh sufficiently factors exacerbating the difficulties of improving the works and exploiting their comparative advantage. In a revealing report of April 1943 on the decidedly high *Selbstkosten* at Rombach, the plant administration offered "without reservation" an account of how the situation had become so "unsatisfactory."[40] Initial fears that the dilapidated condition of the works in 1941 would lead to a high rate of mechanical failure were not only borne out but surpassed. While virtually every aspect of the operations turned out to require attention—"the Martin furnaces, control panels, gas machinery, electrical motors, rail trackage and engines, boilers, etc."—certain problems so impaired productivity that they, more than other factors, accounted for what the report called the "poor exploitation" of the Rombach works. The condition of the steelworks supercharger, for example, had been permitted to deteriorate so badly that on 8 April it failed catastrophically. The entire Rombach plant shut down for eleven hours, a financial and logistical calamity for a major steelworks. And it was no wonder that such incidents came about, the report continued: the underlying rot in the infrastructure and machinery made large-scale stoppages inevitable. The newest lathe in the machine shop, for example, was already thirty years old. As the report argued, "We must come to terms with these issues before anything else, as we cannot . . . cut back on our improvement campaign for critical reasons of the war effort."[41]

In addition to the decrepit physical infrastructure, the labor force presented another insurmountable hurdle to Flick's plans for Rombach. Here the convergence with the general situation in the Germany war economy is most evident. The Third Reich suffered serious manpower shortages from the mid-1930s onward; these notwithstanding, the difficulty of allocating labor to crucial industries was complicated by the adverse conditions of wartime. Foreign workers were not a straightforward alternative: the Allied bomber offensive, the rationing of food and basic goods, and poor living conditions, to say nothing of the ideological outlook of the Nazi state, worked against initiatives to induce laborers from elsewhere in Europe to work in German industries. The expedient to which Nazi Germany resorted was forced labor in its many incarnations.[42] A loose definition of forced labor would include every worker in the entire German economy: to deal with shortages, which were made worse by progressively more extensive military conscription during the war, the government enacted laws preventing even the most native German workers from moving between jobs. By no reasonable standard, however, could their situation be compared with those of foreigners compelled to work in German war industries, as compared with the few who voluntarily complied. But even among those compelled to work one finds important variances: some, primarily western Europeans, retained basic rights and enjoyed limited legal protections and recourse to rudimentary grievance procedures, while others were slave laborers, and still others what some historians have called "less-than-slave labor," meaning that the labor authority in question had no stake in their survival or actively sought to eradicate them.[43] The distinctions between different types of forced labor are critical to understanding the nature of labor in Nazi Germany generally, if only for the light they shed on Nazi social and racial typologies, the economic circumstances of the war economy, and the heterogeneous character of personal experience under the regime.

As was true for almost every economic entity in the Third Reich, the Nazi regime limited the discretion of the Flick concern or the individual plants within it to deal with labor questions. Since the advent of labor shortages in the mid-1930s, an elaborate system of allocation based on the requirements of individual plants and an oversight board involving officials from a range of agencies doled out manpower largely independent of a firm's preferences. By the time the German drive into the Soviet Union had stagnated, the "Decree on the Preservation of Manpower in the War Economy," issued in May 1942, spelled the end of what little autonomy remained to firms in disposing of labor as they saw fit.[44] The decree granted the Reich Labor Office complete authority to determine which workers were to be detailed to a given location, the relations that obtained between employers and a workforce, and to a substantial extent, under what specific physical circumstances they would work and live. The decree also stipulated stiff punishments for transgressors, namely workers who fled their assigned positions or employers who released or hired them without the consent of the authorities. In the case of Rombach, responsibility for assigning workers and defining the terms of their employment lay with the Labor Office of the civil administration and the German Labor Front, which arranged for the care and feeding of workers in other respects.[45] The company retained responsibility only for housing workers: an internal listing of major investment programs at Rombach as of August 1943 included RM 950,000 for residential camps for German and eastern workers assigned there.[46]

For the administration of Rombach, the challenge of securing a competent labor force was worsened by the circumstances of the local administration and the war economy. As described in the first chapter, the German administration of Lorraine expelled many French citizens who did not hail originally from Moselle or Lorraine or whose loyalty to France was considered primary.[47] The intention was to replace them with Germans, with the twin purpose of safeguarding the operation of the economy in the German interest and changing the demographic face of Lorraine. As a result, 48 engineers called into French military service in June 1940 could not return to Lorraine and their civilian jobs in the Rombach plant after the French military collapse. The civil administration further mandated the expulsion of 266 personnel for various reasons between 1940 and 1944, while 327 workers were deported to Germany for industrial work there and a further 818 were conscripted into the Wehrmacht. Under optimal conditions, Rombach employed between 6,000 and 7,000 workers and around 600 clerical staff. By late 1941, the Flick concern had managed to boost the labor force to 5,388 workers and 306 clerical staff. The number of workers increased during the war, but numbers alone say nothing about their suitability for work in a steel plant. A report from late 1944 listed the total nontechnical workforce at 6,200, of whom 25 percent were women and young girls and a substantial proportion were under sixteen.[48] Furthermore, an alarmingly high proportion of the native workers, on whom the efficiency of the plant depended, were well advanced in years, which led to a relatively high number of natural deaths, accidents, and a sickness rate far beyond those found at a normally staffed steelworks. According to the works administration, at no point did the number of technical personnel, meaning engineers and industry specialists, approach the number required to maintain the plant properly, to say nothing of using it fully.[49]

Guidelines formulated early in the war by Hermann Röchling in his role as supervisor of the steel industry in Lorraine asserted the responsibility of trustees for the well-being of the legacy workers they inherited.[50] Even in this category, the labor force at Rombach was inferior. By all accounts, the Flick concern took over in 1941 a labor force that was comparatively understrength and inefficient. A Rombach plant official reported that the French plant administration in the interwar period had earned the dubious distinction of paying the lowest wages in the industry, inducing a flight by the most able workers to other nearby plants, notably Hagendingen. Coupled with this preexisting handicap, the disruptions of the war's first year served to undercut further the morale of an already apathetic collection of workers.[51] In its April 1943 report to the concern, the plant administration arrived at a highly critical assessment of the "mentality of the Rombach workers."[52] The report noted that the overall wage-to-productivity ratio (*Verdienstverhältnisse*) had improved somewhat as a result of a stringent wage policy initiated by Gauleiter Bürckel and a significant lengthening of the work week. However, as compared with the type of productivity gains made when workers function more effectively and technology expedites their efforts, this is a poor measure of the actual state of the labor force. Indeed, the report continues by noting that, the wage-to-productivity ratio notwithstanding, the labor situation generally had deteriorated badly since the Flick concern had reinstituted production at Rombach. Most of the French workers were regarded as "thoroughly contaminated" by Communist sensibilities, while the Italian, Russian, and Polish workers were believed to resist all efforts to reconcile them to their station through "National Socialist economic leadership." English radio broadcasts describing Germany's crumbling military situation were widely heard, feeding the workers' apparently fervent hopes that German defeat was imminent. Nearly three years of German administration in Lorraine had done more on the whole to rile the population than pacify it. Forced expulsions and high-profile resettlements of ethnic French nationals combined with the ham-fisted social policies of Bürckel's administration in Metz to make the workforce a ripe target for underground Communist and Allied propaganda.[53]

To make matters worse, the German administration in Lorraine engaged in an impractical series of labor "equalizations," whereby workers were shifted from one plant to the next for housing purposes and the most qualified native Lorrainers were shipped to Germany for work in the steel mills of the Altreich. Rombach thus lost 500 *Stammarbeitern* to plants in the Saar and received in return Soviet prisoners of war, who were replaced only two months later—before any meaningful job training could take place—by 600 almost wholly ineffectual "eastern workers" (*Ostarbeiter*) between the ages of 14 and 18. Rombach also gave up a further 500 local workers to nearby plants while taking in 360 from the nearby Mövern plant, which was shut down due to the acute shortage of coking coal. Such dislocations rendered any sustained production or continuity of training practices impossible. The results of such policies were predictably baleful. For these reasons, the works administration understandably ranked the labor situation as the single greatest problem confounding production at Rombach.[54]

The consequences of the deteriorating German war effort, especially the effects of Allied strategic bombing on the transportation system, had direct implications for Rombach's operations and served to bring home the hazards of wartime industrial expansion and acquisition. As this brief survey suggests, operations at Rombach suffered from the same problems that plagued the German steel industry even before 1939 but that became much worse with Allied bombing and wartime labor problems. Chronic shortages of coking coal, a complicated investment environment, and constant official supervision of production programs all contributed to the difficulty of doing business in Lorraine. In the course of negotiations in May

1944 over one of the most ambitious investment programs envisioned for the Rombach works to date, Otto Flick called attention to the impossible bottleneck that had developed in the supply of coking coal as a result of heavy Allied strategic bombing of Germany's transportation networks. The plant administration had been forced to reckon with constantly declining rates of delivery, with only a fraction of the necessary amount coming from the Ruhr and none at all from northern France by mid-1944. Mere weeks before the onset of the most intensive Allied air interdiction campaign to date in support of the Normandy landings, he wrote that "I cannot imagine that we'll receive enough coke in the coming months . . . in any event we are operating presently with only three furnaces," a utilization rate of only 37.5 percent. Again, Flick argued his case for acquiring Rombach to the authorities in part on the basis of his concern's ability to keep it supplied with coke from his Harpen works. Given the extent to which the latter assumption turned out to be inaccurate by 1944, it was with grim comfort that the younger Flick could point out that "one must not overlook that we have not yet purchased the works."[55] Of equal significance for the poor value of the acquisition was the fact that the Nazi regime eventually opted to retain control of the ore supply in Lorraine instead of turning it over to the steelworks situated there. Flick's assessment of the benefits of acquiring Rombach turned in part on the prospect of low *Selbstkosten,* or the internal cost to a firm of producing a given quantity of steel, which was based on the direct access to ore pits that many of the Lorraine plants historically enjoyed. In compelling the Lorraine mills to purchase ore on the domestic market in the same manner as plants elsewhere, the regime eliminated the cost benefit and made the acquisition of Rombach a losing proposition for Flick.[56]

If the Flick concern never succeeded in overcoming the problems it inherited with the trusteeship of Rombach, it did enjoy a degree of success in producing armaments and overseeing the production of armaments elsewhere. In his postwar testimony, Flick claimed not to know "with certainty" whether Rombach produced munitions for the Nazi war effort. According to him, the works produced rails, iron bars, and rolled steel for both the German and French markets, the latter in his estimation accounting for some 30 to 40 percent of its finished output, along with cement.[57]

TABLE 1. PRODUCTION OF UNFINISHED STEEL AT THE ROMBACH WORKS, 1942–1943 (IN MILLIONS OF TONS)

1943	January	54,539
	February	49,604
	March	53,222
	April	47,022
	May	52,220
	June	51,075
	July	50,121
1944	January	49,931
	February	47,086
	March	47,374
	April	42,387
	May	37,174
	June	42,046

Source: BA-R 13I/550, RVE, Hauptabteilung Statistik, Rohstahl, Entwicklung der Erzeugung nach Werken bzw. Konzernen; from Bähr et al., *Flick Konzern*, 458. [Note: Discrepancy in years appears in reference.]

Although the evidence does not reveal how much of the plant's output consisted of finished armaments, however, it does point to armaments contracts that required rather sizable investments in equipment and entailed a notable degree of oversight from Reich and military authorities. The plant's level of output would probably not have escaped his notice, making his postwar claim of ignorance seem improbable.[58] In addition, correspondence addressed to him by his son, among others, brought to his attention Rombach's direct oversight of French munitions firms working on German military contracts as well as important details of its own production.[59] At the end of January 1943, officials from the Army Ordnance Office approached Odilo Burkart in the interest of securing the participation of the Flick concern, through the Rombach works, in a program to sponsor French firms working on contracts for the German war machine. On the basis of a "general agreement" between the Ministry for Armaments and

Munitions and the Vichy authorities to apportion such contracts among a number of French firms, the Ordnance Office sought to have the Rombach works supervise production in four or five French munitions plants. The plants had already negotiated the contracts through the headquarters of the German occupation in Paris. It was presumably thought that by bundling the contracts together and assigning some degree of risk for their fulfillment to a German sponsoring firm, greater efficiencies in production could be realized at lower cost to the authorities. In addition to developing privileged supplier relationships, the supervising firms would in turn receive some proportion of the earnings.[60] Burkart quickly placed the officials in direct touch with Otto-Ernst Flick, who kept his father notified as to the status of the program.[61] As production of anti-armor munitions was then considered an urgent priority and required electrical furnaces, Rombach was to undertake a crash program to erect the additional electrical furnace capacity and begin manufacture of the specialized steel required.[62] These initiatives soon mushroomed into finished munitions and the preparation of intermediate products for assembly elsewhere. A detailed memorandum of early 1943 outlined a program of munitions production of noteworthy breadth and depth at Rombach and by firms it supervised, which included the fabrication of munitions, weaponry, vehicles, and finished aircraft components.[63]

Rombach's most notable client in this regard appears to have been a large munitions plant called Champagne sur Seine, which became the focus of the chief representative of the plant's Paris office in late 1943. The operation was significant enough to warrant a visit by a delegation of military luminaries that included the chief engineer of the Army Ordnance Office and General Wilhelm von Leeb, the field marshal in command of Army Group North during Operation Barbarossa, who had been forced into semiretirement after the siege of Leningrad. In the course of the tour, Leeb commented very favorably on Rombach's supervision of production at Champagne sur Seine and expressed a desire to see the plant take up similar responsibilities for other French firms. In his report to his father, the younger Flick confessed that he had been unable under the circumstances to admit to the general that Rombach had neither the additional steel required to supply more firms nor the personnel required to staff them.[64]

Overall, the wartime trusteeship of Rombach turned out to be a money-losing venture for the Flick concern.[65] By the time Rombach was evacuated by order of the military authorities during the night of 31 August–1 September 1944, the Flick concern had little of value to show for its years of trusteeship aside from some 8.345 million French francs in large bills from its Paris marketing accounts, which it trucked to Sulzbach-Rosenberg for safekeeping.[66] Any profits the plant realized were swallowed up by the maintenance and improvement of the works, the costs of which appear to have far exceeded earnings; the joint institutional shareholders, Harpen and Maxhütte, did not receive a single dividend before operations ceased in late 1944.[67] The concern's indirect sponsorship of French munitions firms through the Rombach works likewise failed to bring any tangible benefit, with the proceeds of those ventures going to maintenance of the physical plant of the sponsored firms. In view of these facts, it seems that Flick was better at maneuvering for advantage in a bureaucratic spoils system than he was at anticipating the outcome of events in either the short or long term. To be fair, however, it seems likely that he would have reaped considerable economic gain from his control of Rombach had the war turned out differently.

Conclusion

orraine was of marginal significance to Nazi strategic ambitions before World War II, despite its enormous potential value to the economy. Its chief appeal lay in vast iron-ore deposits that held out the possibility of an autarkic and efficient steel industry to provide for the war effort and long-term German economic dominance on the European continent. Following the defeat of France, the Nazi regime considered Lorraine a part of Germany and instituted an occupation regime that sought eventually to incorporate the region's economy into that of Germany. This intention dovetailed with the ambitions of the German steel industry, which saw in the production centers of Lorraine a solution both to its high-cost dependence on imported iron ore and the challenges presented by the Reichswerke Hermann Göring, the pretext for the construction of which had been the need to draw on domestic ores for the war effort. An effort by the Reichswerke itself to acquire assets in Lorraine and waxing state involvement in the economy constituted a compelling motive for an industrialist like Friedrich Flick to reinforce his position through a toehold in Lorraine.[1] In addition, Flick had to reckon with the possibility that the Reichswerke, to feed its own expansion, would soon demand that he surrender a portion of his coal base, the surplus of which was greater than that of any other concern. Acquiring a steel mill like Rombach in the Lorraine ore district would absorb a noteworthy percentage of his coal surplus and possibly deflect the state's attention from his concern. Viewed in this light, it is reasonable to assume that Flick would not have sought to acquire Rombach had it not been for the war launched by the Nazi regime and the pressures exerted on his decision-making by the rise of the Reichswerke. His effort was, in other words, a direct response to the specific environment created by the regime, even if it unfolded for reasons specific to his concern and its interests.

Although Flick made much in postwar testimony of his refusal to contemplate acquisition of the Rombach works before Germany signed a final peace treaty with France, his campaign to win the trusteeship and negotiate the terms by which he would operate the plant reflected a clear intention to control it as a wholly owned asset and in as profitable a manner as possible. Indeed, Flick's negotiations with the authorities over the issue of asset depreciation and amortization make sense only in terms of a proactive, if indirect campaign to convince them that the trusteeship would be profitable only if ownership were assumed. Indeed, given Hanneken's adamant refusal to entertain demands for outright ownership, it is reasonable to conclude that Flick's postwar claims were disingenuous and made solely for the benefit of his defense. This point is driven home by his concern's administration of the works before evacuating them in late 1944. The Flick concern made investments too large and improvements too fundamental to be made up by short-term profits. Flick clearly regarded the works as integral to his concern and would have seized the chance to own them outright.

The presence in Flick's decision-making of factors beyond those implied by narrow corporate profit-seeking complicate interpretations of his motivation in acquiring Rombach and running it. The historical analysis of corporate actors in the Nazi period requires recognition, as Harold James puts it, that "there was nothing very usual about German business at that time."[2] In view of the regime's distortion of essential market mechanisms, especially prices, interest rates, and dividends, it is implausible to speak of a profit motive underlying corporate decision-making:

> Profits in themselves made no sense, but capturing the political process that then increasingly shaped economic outcomes rather certainly did. Instead of competing in a market for market share, businesses competed for influence in a political market that functioned on its own terms and logic. ... This was especially true when the political market was shaken up by the German conquests and when new opportunities became apparent.[3]

James' account of business strategies under the anomalous circumstances of Nazi rule accounts for why Flick pursued more advantageous terms for his trusteeship and invested such great sums in Rombach even as Germany's position worsened and when eventual German defeat was apparent. Under the Nazi regime the terms of economic success changed. As the Reichswerke demonstrated, power and influence mattered as much if not more than profits or efficiency, and both were served in Flick's case by the acquisition and maintenance of the Rombach works. In addition, Flick felt his reputation as an entrepreneur to be at stake. As he put it in his postwar trial in connection to his decision to continue investing in Rombach even after it was clear Germany had lost the war, "I didn't want anybody to say that I had used a trusteeship over a foreign plant in order to use it for our personal advantage and to the disadvantage of the real owners . . . there are also conceptions concerning prestige and concerning the reputation of the entrepreneur."[4] How seriously he took his own "prestige" and "reputation" in view of his participation in the Aryanization campaigns is an open question. All the same, quite apart from the Nazi regime's having created the conditions that made expansion seem prudent, Flick persisted in his upkeep of Rombach as a way of providing for future possibilities in a postwar environment driven by conventional market mechanisms.

In considering Flick's efforts to take over and manage a major steelworks in Lorraine, this study undermines the notion that a distinctively Nazi approach to economic issues guided the expropriation and exploitation of the Lorraine steel industry. Expedience and opportunism governed the approach of senior German economic officials and industrialists alike, meaning that both were guided in their actions and decisions more by a conception of their diverse parochial interests than by a clear, collective understanding of what constituted a "National Socialist" solution to the issues they confronted. Many were committed Nazis, to be sure, and made decisions informed by priorities that derived from their ideological orientation, such as efforts to expel foreign and Jewish elements entirely from the economy of Lorraine or the autocratic appointment by a single Nazi official of trustees to manage the steel firms of the region. However, such actions or decisions never occurred in a vacuum; other interested parties advanced countervailing or alternative policies that derived frequently from different orientations, and those orientations impacted the final shape of economic relations in frequently decisive ways. As Peter Hayes has put it,

> The diffusion of governmental authority nearly matched that of industrial interests. As of 1939, the contenders for control over parts or all of German production included the Ministry of Economics and Labor, the Four Year Plan organization and its five principal subdivisions, the ordnance offices of the three armed services, and the Military Economy and Armaments Staff of the High Command under General [Georg] Thomas. During the ensuing six years, the names of the claimants to power changed, the lack of coordination among them persisted.[5]

In Flick's machinations and the context in which they took place, one can point to an apparent consensus on broad fundamentals, such as the intention to incorporate Lorraine into a contiguous German economic area and exploit it on behalf of primarily German interests. However, those fundamentals were not deep enough to justify the notion of uniquely "National Socialist solutions" to occupation policy and exploitation. Many of the features of the exploitation process apparent here, although not its impetus, need not necessarily have derived from Nazi economic ideas. Autarkic policies on a continental scale can be viewed as a strategic necessity, pursued by the regime to counteract the vulnerabilities of dependence on overseas sources of raw materials; that the strategic necessity for those policies was rooted in an ideological impetus cannot be disputed. Likewise, the Nazi regime's willingness to aid private German firms like that of Friedrich Flick in subduing its European rivals and securing market share and assets in the occupied territories seems practically similar to French attempts to overturn German dominance of certain market segments in the wake of World War I, even if those attempts were rooted in different ideological arguments.[6] This is not to suggest that the Nazi regime pursued an agenda, however well or poorly, indistinguishable from those of other nation-states in wartime. Rather, in considering Nazi plans and policies one must be mindful of a key characteristic of the regime, namely its success in harnessing apparently rational means to the pursuit of murderously irrational ends. In other words, certain features of the Nazi economic program in Lorraine appear consistent with the predictable imperatives of wartime mobilization (whereas others, such as the wholesale deportation or extermination of ethnic minorities, were clearly not). In the absence of an integrated history of German economic and occupation policy in Western Europe, therefore, overarching reliance on the idea of a distinctive Nazi New Order to account for economic policy seems questionable, or at least requires the historian to distinguish between those aspects of Nazi policies that tended to the efficient use of resources and those that contradicted it.

The recent historical research of which this study is a part has lent fresh importance to the pursuit by industrialists or minor functionaries of their localized interests in defining the economic landscape of Nazi Germany. Doing so has recast the terms in which responsibility for the activities of the Nazi regime has been traditionally cast. The importance of individual firms or businessmen is rendered especially acute by the scale of Flick's activities and the importance of his concern for the war that the regime took to be its principal mission. In this sense, and regardless of whatever else he might have done short of abandoning his position, he was by default institutionally more complicit than most other industrialists, whose activities were frequently much narrower in scope, of lesser significance for the Nazi war machine, or filtered through a system of corporate ownership and responsibility that mitigated their roles. Friedrich Flick is not, then, a typical case of an industrialist active under the Nazi regime who then left behind a legacy of controversy over his activities. By virtue of the extraordinary range of his interests, the choices he confronted were often different than those facing most others, and his responses to those choices were necessarily conditioned by the demands of managing a concern essential to the Nazi government's pursuit of its ambitions. For this reason, one must generalize only with the greatest caution from his experiences to the state of industry broadly under the Nazi regime.

NOTES

Introduction

1. The Flick concern has been the subject of much recent scholarship. Definitive is the new collaborative study by Johannes Bähr, Axel Drecoll, Bernhard Gotto, Kim C. Priemel, and Harald Wixforth, eds., *Der Flick Konzern im Dritten Reich* (München: Oldenbourg Wissenschaftsverlag, 2008), which features diverse contributions on a range of the firm's operations and corporate culture; and Kim Christian Priemel, *Flick: Eine Konzerngeschichte vom Kaiserreich bis zur Bundesrepublik* (Göttingen: Wallstein, 2007).

2. Eckart Teichert, *Autarkie und Großraumwirtschaft in Deutschland 1930–1939: Außenwirtschaftspolitische Konzeptionen zwischen Wirtschaftskrise und Zweitem Weltkrieg* (München: Oldenbourg, 1984), 390; also Horst Kahrs, "Von der 'Großraumwirtschaft' zur 'neuen Ordnung': Zur strategischen Orientierung der deutschen Eliten 1932–1945," in *Modelle für ein deutsches Europa: Ökonomie und Herrschaft im Großwirtschaftsraum*, ed. Horst Kahrs and Götz Aly (Berlin: Rotbuch, 1992), 9–28.

3. Hans-Erich Volkmann, "L'importance économique de la Lorraine pour le IIIe Reich," *Revue d'histoire de la deuxième guerre mondiale* 120 (1980), 69–93.

4. Paul Erker, "Aufbruch zu neuen Paradigmen: Unternehmensgeschichte zwischen sozialgeschichtlicher und betriebswirtschaftlicher Erweiterung," *Archiv für Sozialgeschichte* 37 (1997), 321–65.

5. A leading example of "modernization" analysis, which places developments in the Nazi era in the broader sweep of German economic development, is the work of Knut Borchardt, most notably selections from his *Perspectives on Modern German Economic History and Policy* (New York: Cambridge University Press, 1991); for a definitive Marxist-Leninist appreciation, see Dietrich Eichholtz, *Geschichte der deutschen Kriegswirtschaft 1939–1945*, 2 vols. (Berlin: Akademie Verlag, 1965–89); the best analysis of economic policy in the light of Nazi ideology is Avraham Barkai, *Nazi Economics: Ideology, Theory, and Policy* (New Haven: Yale University Press, 1990).

6. Alan Milward, *The New Order and the French Economy* (Oxford: Oxford University Press, 1970); the same case, stated more succinctly, can be found in idem, "German Economic Policy towards France 1942–1944," in *Studies in International History*, ed. K. Bourne and D. C. Watts (London: Longmans Press, 1967).

7. Milward, *The New Order*, 33. The original statement of Milward's interpretation of the German war economy before 1942, which drew on the research of Nicholas Kaldor of the United States Strategic Bombing Survey and became axiomatic in much subsequent historiography, is found in idem, *The German Economy at War* (London: Athlone Press, 1965); idem, "Der Einfluß ökonomischer und nicht–ökonomischer Faktoren auf die Strategie des Blitzkrieges," in *Wirtschaft und Rüstung am Vorabend des Zweiten Weltkrieges*, ed. Friedrich Forstmeier and Hans-Erich Volkmann (Düsseldorf: Droste, 1975), 189–201. Consistent with recent research on the German war economy, according to Alfred Mierzejewski, Milward has largely abandoned his claims on the relationship between German operational strategy and economic mobilization, which lay at the heart of the notion of a Blitzkrieg economy: Mierzejewski review of Neil Gregor, *Daimler-Benz in the Third Reich* (New Haven: Yale University Press, 1998), http://eh.net/bookreviews/library/0156.shtml, accessed 12 July 2006.

8. Timothy Mason, *Social Policy in the Third Reich: The Working Class and the "National Community"* (Providence/Oxford: Berg, 1993), 182, 207.

9. Rolf-Dieter Müller, "Die Mobilisierung der deutschen Wirtschaft für Hitlers Kriegsführung," in *Organisierung und Mobilmachung des deutschen Machtbereichs: Kriegsverwaltung, Wirtschaft und Personelle Ressourcen 1939–1941*, ed. B. Kroener, R.-D. Müller, and H. Umbreit, *Das Deutsche Reich und der Zweite Weltkrieg*, vol. 5.1, ed. Militärgeschichtlichen Forschungsamt (Stuttgart: Deutsche Verlags-Anstalt, 1988), 491.

10. See the collected articles in sections III and IV of R. J. Overy, *War and Economy in the Third Reich* (Oxford: Oxford University Press, 1994); see also the modification of Overy's assertions regarding the employment of women and levels of civilian consumption in Mark Harrison, "Resource Mobilization for World War II: The USA, U.K., U.S.S.R., and Germany, 1938–1945," *The Economic History Review* 41 (1988), 187, notes 34 and 35.

11. On this aspect of Milward's argument, see Richard Tilly's review of his work in *The Journal of Economic History* 34 (1974), 513; more broadly, the same argument is advanced more forcefully in the cases of the electrical, transportation, and credit sectors of the economy in Gerald Ambrosius, "Was war eigentlich 'nationalsozialistisch' an den Regulierungsansätzen der dreißiger Jahre?," in *Wirtschaftsordnung, Staat und Unternehmen: Neue Forschungen zur Wirtschaftsgeschichte des Nationalsozialismus. Festschrift für Dietmar Petzina zum 65. Geburtstag*, ed. Werner Abelshauser, Jan-Otmar Hesse, and Werner Plumpe (Essen: Klartext, 2003), 41–60.

12. Milward, *The New Order*, 100; this issue has enlivened debate over the Nazi economy considerably of late: see Ambrosius, "Was war eigentlich 'nationalsozialistisch' an den Regulierungsansätzen der dreißiger Jahre?," in *Wirtschaftsordnung*, 40–60.

13. The best exposition of this view, which reserves a dominant role for Hitler, is found in Karl-Dietrich Bracher, "The Stages of Totalitarian Integration (*Gleichschaltung*)," in *Republic to Reich: The Making of the Nazi Revolution*, ed. Hajo Holborn (New York: Vintage Books, 1973); more radical "structuralist" accounts relegating Hitler to the role of a virtual agent of complex power coalitions abound.

14. Gerhard Weinberg, "Germany's War for World Conquest and the Extermination of the Jews," *Holocaust and Genocide Studies* 10 (1996), 119–33.

15. See Ralf Banken, "Kurzfristiger Boom oder langfristiger Forschungsschwerpunkt? Die neuere deutsche Unternehmensgeschichte und die Zeit des Nationalsozialismus," *Geschichte in Wissenschaft und Unterricht* 56 (2005), 183–96.

16. See the characterization of this period as "the first stage in the general crisis of capitalism": Rudolf Berthold, *Geschichte der Produktivekräfte in Deutschland 1917/8 bis 1945* (Berlin: Akademie Verlag, 1988), 566.

17. See the study by Henry Ashby Turner Jr., *German Big Business and the Rise of Hitler* (Oxford: Oxford University Press, 1985).

18. Reinhard Neebe, "Die Industrie und der 30 Januar 1933," in *Nationalsozialistische Diktatur 1933–1945. Eine Bilanz*, ed. K.-D. Bracher, Manfred Funke, and H.-A. Jacobsen (Bonn: Bundeszentrale für Politische Bildung, 1983), 155.

19. On resistance and nonconformity, see Wilhelm Treue, "Widerstand von Unternehmern und Nationalökonomen," in *Der Widerstand gegen den Nationalsozialismus: Die Deutsche Gesellschaft und der Widerstand gegen Hitler*, ed. Jürgen Schmädeke and Peter Steinbach (München: R. Piper, 1985), 917–36.

20. Michael Schneider, "Nationalsozialistische Durchdringung von Staat, Wirtschaft und Gesellschaft. Zur Sozialgeschichte des Dritten Reiches," *Archiv für Sozialgeschichte* 31 (1991), 514–57.

21. Alan S. Milward, "Bericht," in *Industrielles System und politische Entwicklung in der Weimarer Republik*, vol. 1, ed. H. Mommsen, D. Petzina, and B. Weisbrod (Düsseldorf: Droste, 1974), 55.

22. Peter Hayes, "Big Business and 'Aryanization' in Germany," *Jahrbuch für Antisemitismusforschung* 3 (1994), 254–81.

23. See, for example, Hervé Joly, *Großunternehmer in Deutschland: Soziologie einer industriellen Elite 1933–1989* (Leipzig: Leipziger Universitätsverlag, 1998).

24. A noteworthy recent exception is Peter Hayes, *From Cooperation to Complicity: Degussa in the Third Reich* (Cambridge: Cambridge University Press, 2004), which is remarkable for its grasp of internal corporate procedures and priorities.

25. Paul Kluke, "Nationalsozialistische Volkstumspolitik in Elsaß-Lothringen 1940 bis 1945," in *Zur Geschichte und Problematik der Demokratie. Festschrift für Hans Herzfeld* (Berlin: Duncker und Humbolt, 1958), 619–36.

Chapter 1. Nazi German Plans and Policies in Lorraine

1. For background to this issue, see the study by Dieter Wolfanger, "Die nationalsozialistische Politik in Lothringen (1940–1945)" (Saarbrücken, Univ. Diss., 1977); idem, *Nazification de la Lorraine mosellane* (Sarreguemines: Editions Pierrons, 1982); also Adrien Prinz, *Chronique Lorraine, 1940–1944* (Paris, 1945); and F.-Yves Le Moigne, *Moselle et mosellans dans la Seconde Guerre mondiale* (Metz: Editions Serpenoise, 1983).

2. *Monologe im Führer-Hauptquartier, 1941–1944*, ed. Werner Jochmann (Hamburg: A. Knaus, 1980), 55 (8–11 August 1941); see the summary by Michael Salewski, "National Socialist Ideas on Europe," in *Documents on the History of European Integration*, vol. 1, *Continental Plans for European Union 1939–1945*, ed. Walter Lipgens (Berlin: De Gruyter, 1985), 37–178.

3. See Paul Kluke, "Nationalsozialistische Europaideologie," *Vierteljahrshefte für Zeitgeschichte* 3 (1955), 240–75, who argues that Hitler's ambition was the establishment of a power-political Germanic empire, not a unified European civilization; also Lothar Gruchmann, *Nationalsozialistische Grossraumordnung: Die Konstruktion einer "deutschen Monroe-Doktrin"* (Stuttgart: Deutsche Verlagsanstalt, 1962); and Birgit Kletzin, *Europa aus Rasse und Raum: Die nationalsozialistische Idee der Neuen Ordnung* (Münster: Lit, 2000).

4. Karl-Dietrich Bracher, *Die deutsche Diktatur: Enstehung, Struktur, Folgen des Nationalsozialismus* (Köln: Kiepenheuer und Witsch, 1970), 438; see also Peter Hüttenberger, "Nationalsozialistische Polykratie," *Geschichte und Gesellschaft* 2 (1976), 417–42.

5. Eberhard Jäckel, *Hitler's World View: A Blueprint for Power* (Cambridge: Harvard University Press, 1981), 35–37; Axel Kuhn, *Hitlers außenpolitisches Programm: Entstehung und Entwicklung 1919–1933* (Stuttgart: Klett, 1970); Jochen Thies, *Architekt der Weltherrschaft: Die Endziele Hitlers* (Düsseldorf: Droste, 1976).

6. Norman Rich, *Hitler's War Aims: Ideology, the Nazi State, and the Course of Expansion* (New York: Norton, 1973), 133; on the character of German administration and economic exploitation in those regions, see the recent study by Robert Bohn, *Reichskommissariat Norwegen: "Nationalsozialistische Neuordnung" und Kriegswirtschaft* (München: Oldenbourg, 2000); and Philip Giltner, *"In the Friendliest Manner": German-Danish Economic Cooperation during the Nazi Occupation 1940–1945* (New York: Peter Lang Publishing, 1998).

7. Harald Winkel, "Die wirtschaftlichen Beziehungen Deutschlands zu Dänemark in den Jahren der Besetzung 1940–1945," in *Probleme der nationalsozialistischen Wirtschaftspolitik*, ed. F. W. Henning (Berlin: Duncker und Humblot, 1976), 119–74; note the comments of Ambassador Hemmen, head

of the Reich economic delegation to the Armistice Commission with France after 1940, who claimed in industrial matters to have "always followed a line which had been much more successful in preserving the true economic interests of both sides on a commercial basis." *NMT*, NI-6767, vol. 8, 122.

8. Reginald Phelps, "Hitler als Parteiredner im Jahre 1920," *Vierteljahrshefte für Zeitgeschichte* 2 (1963), 305.

9. Hitler's proposals at this point differed little from those of radical revisionists generally, who called for the abolition of Versailles and restoration of the frontiers of 1914. See Günter Schubert, *Anfänge nationalsozialistische Außenpolitik* (Köln: Verlag Wissenschaft und Politik, 1963). He even declared in 1920 that an alliance with the Soviet Union might be possible were the Jewish influence there eliminated. See Phelps, "Hitler," 308.

10. Adolf Hitler, *Mein Kampf*, trans. Ralph Manheim (Boston: Houghton Mifflin, 1943), 549.

11. Adolf Hitler, *Hitlers Zweites Buch. Ein Dokument aus dem Jahr 1928*, with introduction and commentary by Gerhard Weinberg (Stuttgart: Deutsche Verlags Anstalt, 1961), 103. The best survey of Hitler's uneven attitudes toward France remains Eberhard Jäckel, *Frankreich in Hitlers Europa: Die deutsche Frankreichpolitik im Zweiten Weltkrieg* (Stuttgart: Deutsche Verlags Anstalt, 1966), 13–32.

12. A fuller account of Hitler's approach to the question of Alsace-Lorraine is to be found in Lothar Kettenacker, *Nationalsozialistische Volkstumspolitik im Elsaß* (Stuttgart: Deutsche Verlags Anstalt, 1973), 32–44. The interpretation rendered here derives substantially from Kettenacker's excellent survey.

13. Hitler, *Mein Kampf*, 675.

14. Hitler, *Zweites Buch*, 194.

15. Hitler, *Mein Kampf*, 636.

16. Hermann Rauschning, *Gespräche mit Hitler* (Wien: Europaverlag, 1973), 43; Wolfgang Hänel, *Hermann Rauschnings "Gespräche mit Hitler"—Eine Geschichtsfälschung* (Ingolstadt: Zeitgeschichtliche Forschungstelle, 1984), has challenged the reliability of Rauschning's recollections by pointing out the impossibility of his having spoken with Hitler enough to have gathered so much material. When used with care, however, Rauschning's account may be used to amplify an understanding of Hitler derived from more reliable evidence. See also Theodor Schieder, *Hermann Rauschnings "Gespräche mit Hitler" als Geschichtsquelle* (Opladen: Westdeutscher Verlag, 1972).

17. See Jäckel, *Frankreich in Hitlers Europa*, 75.

18. Franz Knipping, "Frankreich in Hitlers Außenpolitik 1933–1939," in *Hitler, Deutschland und die Mächte: Materialien zur Außenpolitik des Dritten Reiches*, ed. Manfred Funke (Düsseldorf: Droste Verlag, 1976), 616; Jäckel, *Frankreich in Hitlers Europa*, 24–25. A comprehensive treatment of diplomatic relations

between Nazi Germany and France in the years before 1939 remains to be written: Marie-Luise Recker, *Die Aussenpolitik des Dritten Reiches* (München: R. Oldenbourg, 1990), 75.

19. Manfred Messerschmidt, "Foreign Policy and Preparation for War," in Wilhelm Deist, Manfred Messerschmidt, Hans-Erich Volkmann, and Wolfram Wette, *Germany and the Second World War*, vol. 1, *The Build-up of German Aggression* (Oxford: Oxford University Press, 1990), 582–83.

20. See Wilhelm von Schramm, *Sprich vom Frieden, wenn du Krieg willst: Die psychologischen Offensiven Hitlers gegen die Franzosen 1933 bis 1939* (Mainz: Hase und Kohler, 1973).

21. Andre Francois-Poncet, *The Fateful Years. Memoirs of a French Ambassador in Berlin, 1931–1938* (New York: Harcourt, Brace, 1949), 103.

22. Max Domarus, *Hitler: Speeches and Proclamations 1932–1945: The Chronicle of a Dictatorship*, vol. 2, *1935–1938* (Wauconda, Il: Bolchazy-Carducci, 1992), 768–69; see also Hans-Adolf Jacobsen, *Nationalsozialistische Außenpolitik 1933–1938* (Frankfurt am Main: A. Metzner, 1968), 261.

23. Domarus, *Hitler*, vol. 2, 1155.

24. Ibid., 1185.

25. Ibid., 1260.

26. Domarus, *Hitler*, vol. 3, 1562.

27. Letter of Hitler to French Minister-President Daladier, 27 August 1939, *Akten zur Deutschen Auswärtigen Politik*, Serie D, vol. 7, Document 354; also reproduced in Walter Hofer, *Die Entfesselung des Zweiten Weltkrieges. Eine Studie über die internationalen Beziehungen im Sommer 1939 mit Dokumenten* (Frankfurt am Main: Fischer Bücherei, 1963), 303.

28. Domarus, *Hitler*, vol. 3, 1840.

29. On this point, see Andreas Hillgruber, "Frankreich als Faktor der deutschen Außenpolitik im Jahre 1939" (Franco-German historical symposium in Bonn, 26–29 September 1978); also idem, *Hitlers Strategie: Politik und Kriegführung, 1940–1941* (Frankfurt am Main: Bernhard und Graefe Verlag für Wehrwesen, 1965); Williamson Murray, *The Change in the European Balance of Power, 1938–1939: The Path to Ruin* (Princeton: Princeton University Press, 1984), 129–31.

30. On the course of the German military campaign in the West generally, see Ernest May, *Strange Victory: Hitler's Conquest of France* (New York: Hill and Wang, 2000).

31. Hermann Böhme, *Der deutsche-französische Waffenstillstand im Zweiten Weltkrieg* (Stuttgart: Deutsche Verlags Anstalt, 1966), 297.

32. The armistice treaty is reproduced in ibid., 364ff.

33. Letter from German Foreign Office to Administration of Lorraine, 10 January 1941, NI-2800, RG238 M891/14/1074.

34. Robert Ernst, *Rechenschaftsbericht eines Elsässers* (Berlin: Bernard und Graefe, 1954), 230; Kettenacker, *Nationalsozialistische Volkstumspolitik im Elsaß*, 48.

35. Erlaß des Führers über die vorläufige Verwaltung in Elsaß und Lothringen, 8 February 1940, BA-MA RW4/732.

36. On Bürckel, see Jeremy Noakes, "'Viceroys of the Reich?' *Gauleiters 1925–45*," in *Working Towards the Führer*, ed. Anthony McElligott and Tim Kirk (Manchester: Manchester University Press, 2003), 130–31.

37. See especially Gerhard Kratzsch, *Der Gauwirtschaftsapparat der NSDAP: Menschenführung—"Arisierung"—Wehrwirtschaft im Gau Westfalen-Süd. Eine Studie zur Herrschaftspraxis im totalitären Staat* (Münster: Aschendorff, 1989).

38. For the critical role played in this process by the Gauleiter, see the studies edited by Dieter Rebentisch and Karl Teppe, *Verwaltung contra Menschenführung im Staat Hitlers. Studien zum politisch-administrativen System* (Göttingen: Vandenhoeck und Ruprecht, 1986), 23–32.

39. In addition to Kratzsch (above, note 36), see Frank Bajohr, "The 'Aryanization' of Jewish Companies and German Society: The Example of Hamburg," *International Conference: German Society's Response to Nazi Anti-Jewish Policy 1933–1941*, Yad Vashem, 10–13 February 1995, note 42; idem, "The Beneficiaries of 'Aryanization': Hamburg as a Case Study," *Yad Vashem Studies* 26 (1998), 9–10; a fuller explanation is offered in his book: idem, *"Aryanization" in Hamburg: The Economic Exclusion of Jews and the Confiscation of Their Property in Nazi Germany* (New York: Berghahn Books, 2002), 143–52.

40. Burkhart Müller-Hillebrand, *Das Heer 1933–1945. Entwicklung des organisatorischen Aufbaus,* vol. 1, *Das Heer bis zum Kriegsbeginn* (Darmstadt: E. S. Mittler, 1956), 91; Hans Umbreit, "Nationalsozialistische Expansion 1938–1941: Strukturen der deutschen Besatzungsverwaltungen im Zweiten Weltkrieg," in *Dienst für die Geschichte: Gedenkschrift für Walther Hubatsch, 17 Mai 1915–29 Dezember 1984,* ed. Michael Salewski and Josef Schröder (Göttingen: Muster Schmidt, 1985), 163–86.

41. Jules Anneser, *Vautours sur la Lorraine: Documents inédits sur l'occupation en Lorraine rassemblés et commentés* (Metz : Éditions le Lorraine, 1948), 11.

42. Gliederung der Militärverwaltung in den besetzten Westgebiete, 19 June 1940, BA R1501/5432.

43. Aktenvermerk über die Besprechung im Hauptquartier des Generalfeldmarschall Göring v.19.6.1940, PS-1155, RG238 M891/14/1025; also in *IMT*, XXVII, 29–31.

44. File note of Stuckart, 1 July 1940, BA R1501/5379.

45. Ibid.

46. Ernst, *Rechenschaftsbericht*, 261.

47. File note of Stuckart, 25 September 1940, BA R1501/5379.

48. *Neues Staatsrecht* II, Leipzig 1943, NI-5386, RG238 M891/18/0743.

49. Oberkommando der Wehrmacht—Vorläufige Verwaltung im Elsaß, in Lothringen und im Luxemburg, 8 September 1940, WFA/Abt.L(IV)-147/40, BA-MA RW4/732.

50. Anordnung Hitlers vom 18 October 1940—Ergänzung zum Erlass vom 18 October 1940, BA R1501/5379.

51. Beauftragter für den Vierjahresplan, V.P. 11964/5 vom 2.8.1940, Betr: Deutscher Einfluß bei ausländischen Unternehmen, EC-137, RG238 M891/14/1029–32; also in *Nazi Conspiracy and Aggression*, vol. 7 (Washington, DC: U.S. Government Printing Office, 1946), 309–11; also *Fall 5. Anklageplädoyer, ausgewählte Dokumente Urteil des Flick-Prozesses,* ed. Karl-Heinz Thieleke (Berlin: Deutsche Verlag der Wissenschaften, 1965), 226ff.

52. Wolfram Fischer, *Deutsche Wirtschaftspolitik 1918–1945*, 3rd ed. (Opladen: Leske, 1968), 77–82.

53. Henry Ashby Turner Jr., "Hitlers Einstellung zu Wirtschaft und Gesellschaft vor 1933," *Geschichte und Gesellschaft* 2 (1976), 96; Hayes, *Industry and Ideology*, 71–72, note 10; Avraham Barkai, "Sozialdarwinismus und Antiliberalismus in Hitlers Wirtschaftskonzept: Zu Henry A. Turner Jr., Hitlers Einstellung zu Wirtschaft und Gesellschaft vor 1933," *Geschichte und Gesellschaft* 3 (1977), 406–17.

54. Avraham Barkai, *Nazi Economics: Ideology, Theory, and Policy* (New Haven: Yale University Press, 1990), 34–45.

55. Hayes, *Industry and Ideology*, 72; also the study by Curtis Bajak, "The Third Reich's Corporation Law of 1937" (Dissertation, Yale University, 1986); also the recent study by Markus Albert Diehl, *Von der Marktwirtschaft zur nationalsozialistischen Kriegswirtschaft. Die Transformation der deutschen Wirtschaftsordnung 1933–1945* (Stuttgart: Steiner, 2004).

56. A good brief treatment of the Krupp concern in the Third Reich is Werner Abelshauser, "Rüstungsschmiede der Nation? Der Krupp-Konzern im Dritten Reich und in der Nachkriegszeit 1933 bis 1953," in *Krupp im 20. Jahrhundert: Die Geschichte des Unternehmens vom Ersten Weltkrieg bis zur Gründun der Stiftung,* ed. Lothar Gall (Berlin: Siedler, 2002), 267–472.

57. Quoted in Richard J. Overy, "Multi-Nationals and the Nazi State in Occupied Europe," in idem, *War and Economy in the Third Reich* (Oxford: Oxford University Press, 1994), 318.

58. Ibid., 319–21.

59. Göring's Directive of 19 October 1939 concerning the economic administration of the Occupied Territories, EC-410, RG238 M891/14/096–66; also in *Nazi Conspiracy and Aggression*, vol. 7, 466ff.

60. Raabe's mandate also included substantial tracts of eastern French mining territory by virtue of their importance for the steel industry in Lorraine. See Militärbefehlshaber in Frankreich—Gruppe Bergbau und Kohlenwirtshaft (Wi II A) 1940–1944, Abschlussbericht der Gruppe Bergbau und Kohlenwirtschaft, BA-MA RW35/260.

61. Testimony of Paul Raabe, 11 September 1945, RG238 M891/18/0758–65.

62. See Gerhard Thomas Mollin, *Montankonzerne und "Drittes Reich": Der Gegensatz zwischen Monopolindustrie und Befehlswirtschaft in der deutschen Rüstung und Expansion 1936–1944* (Göttingen: Vandenhoeck & Ruprecht, 1988), 235.

63. Richtlinien für die kommissarischen Verwalter der Eisenhütten von Lothringen und Meurthe-et-Moselle vom 5 Juli 1940, BU-819, RG238 M891/31/0096–99.

64. Deposition of Hans Hahl, PS-2217, 11 September 1945, RG238 M891/14/1114–15.

65. No systematic attempt to classify the many different forms of German occupation policy throughout Europe has yet appeared. The best single perspective is Johannes Bähr and Ralf Banken, "Ausbeutung durch Recht? Einleitende Bemerkungen zum Einsatz des Wirtschaftsrechts in der deutschen Besatzungspolitik 1939–1945," in idem, *Das Europa des "Dritten Reichs": Recht, Wirtschaft, Besatzung* (Frankfurt am Main: Klostermann, 2005), 1–30.

66. Otfried Ulshofer, *Einflussnahme auf Wirtschaftsunternehmungen in den besetzten nord-, west- und südosteuropäischen Ländern während des Zweiten Weltkrieges, insbesondere der Erwerb von Beteiligungen* (Tübingen: Institut für Besatzungsfragen, 1958), 19, 38. Ulshofer discusses the different forms that German influence over foreign enterprises could assume, drawing a distinction between what he calls the sovereign (*hoheitlicher*) and the private civil (*privatrechtlicher*) exertion of influence over occupied territories. Such a distinction is of questionable value, as the author himself admits that private transactions took place within a legal context determined by the occupation authorities and differed little from those defined by sovereign authority. See Wolfanger, "Die nationalsozialistische Politik in Lothringen, 1940–1945," 198.

67. Verordnung über die ordnungsmäßige Geschäftsführung und Verwaltung von Unternehmungen und Betrieben in den besetzten Gebieten (Geschäftsführungsverordnung), 23 June 1940, Nr. 8, *Verordnungsblatt für Lothringen* (1940), 8.

68. Durchführungsverordnung zur Geschäftsführungverordnung, 27 July 1940, Nr. 17, *VbfL* (1940), 15. Along similar lines and of legal importance for later acquisitions of assets by German industrialists was the following: Kommissarische Verwaltungen auf Grund der Geschäftsführungverordnung, 1940–1944, BA RW35/256.

69. Verordnung über die Behandlung des feindlichen Vermögens, 24 November 1941, Nr. 633, *VbfL* (1941), 1010; also Anordnung zur Durchführung der Verordnung über die Behandlung des Feindvermögens, Nr. 634, *VbfL* (1940), 1013, which established an office in Metz tasked expressly with handling the transition of industrial property from enemy to German hands; and Verordnung über die Übernahme und Verwertung des französischen Vermögens in Lothringen, 1 December 1941, *VbfL* (1941), 1044. See also Verordnung über die Anmeldung des volks—und reichsfeindlichen Vermögens in Lothringen, 6 November 1940, *VbfL* (1940), 200.

70. Durchführungsverordnung über das Feindvermögen (5.DVFV)—Aufruf von Beteiligungen, 15 June 1942, Nr. 219, *VbfL* (1942), 298. Note that the Civil Administration imposed similarly firm deadlines on the registration of creditors' claims against French property, along with a promise to recognize any previously outstanding legal debt; see 4. Durchführungsverordnung über das Feindvermögen (4.DVFV)—Forderungsanmeldung, 9 June 1942, Nr. 213, *VbfL* (1942), 294. Whether this promise was fulfilled cannot be established.

Chapter 2. Friedrich Flick and His Activities
under the Nazi Regime before 1940

1. Details regarding Flick's personal history appeared in a pamphlet entitled *Friedrich Flick (Zur Vollendung seines 60. Lebensjahres am 10 Juli 1943)*, NI-3020, *Trials of War Criminals before the Nuernberg Military Tribunals under Control Council Law No. 10*, vol. VI (Washington, DC: U.S. Government Printing Office, 1952), 179–85 (hereafter *TWC*); also RG238 M891/12/0031–39; other noteworthy treatments of Flick include Günter Ogger, *Friedrich Flick der Große* (Bern: Scherz, 1971); Ulrike Hörster-Philipps, *Im Schatten des grossen Geldes. Flick-Konzern und Politik: Weimarer Republik, Drittes Reich, Bundesrepublik* (Köln: Pahl-Rugenstein, 1985); Horst Mönnich, *Labyrinthe der Macht. 3 Geschichten vom Kapital: Stinnes, Thyssen, Flick* (Frankfurt am Main: Umschau Verlag, 1975); more recently, Thomas Ramge, *Die Flicks: Eine deutsche Familiengeschichte um Geld, Macht und Politik* (Frankfurt am Main: Campus, 2004).

2. Felix Pinner, *Deutsche Wirtschaftsführer* (Charlottenburg: Weltbühne, 1924); quoted in Paul Ufermann, *Der deutsche Stahltrust* (Berlin: Verlagsgesellschaft des Allgemeinen Deutschen Gewerkschaftsbundes, 1927), 64.

3. See Überblick über die Steigerung der Rüstungsproduktion des Flick-Konzerns, 9.7.1942, NI-3496, reproduced in Thieleke, *Fall 5*, 113–15; also RG238 M891/17/0170.

4. Flick excepted from his calculations the Mannesmann Works for reasons unstated; speech by Flick, NI-3345, 1 April 1940, RG238 M891/12/0189.

5. Überblick über die Steigerung der Rüstungsproduktion des Flick-Konzerns, 9 July 1942, NI-3496, in Thieleke, *Fall 5*, 113–15; also RG238 M891/17/0170. The principal parts of his steel operations at that time are described as Mitteldeutsche Stahlwerke and Maxhütte.

6. Louis Lochner invokes the label in *Tycoons and Tyrant: German Industry from Hitler to Adenauer* (Chicago: H. Regnery Company, 1954), 51; see also NI-3020, *TWC*, 183; more recently the excellent and comprehensive study by Lisa Stallbaumer, "Strictly Business? The Flick Concern and 'Aryanization': Corporate Expansion in the Nazi Era" (Dissertation, University of Wisconsin–Madison, 1995); much of what follows draws directly on Stallbaumer's study, which ranks among the most authoritative scholarly attempts to date to use the full extent of the documentary record. Most historiography on Flick derives from the former East Germany: Thieleke, *Fall 5*; Klaus Drobisch, "Dokumente zur direkten Zusammenarbeit zwischen Flick-Konzern und Gestapo bei der Unterdrückung der Arbeiter," *Jahrbuch für Wirtschaftsgeschichte* 3 (1963), 211–25; idem, "Flick und die Nazis," *Zeitschrift für Geschichtswissenschaft* 14 (1966), 378–97; idem, "Flick-Konzern und faschistischen Staat, 1933–1939," in *Monopole und Staat in Deutschland, 1917–1945*, ed. Karl Drechsler (Berlin: Akademie Verlag, 1966), 183–92.

7. Stallbaumer, "Strictly Business?," 93.

8. On Flick's early acquisitions and business activities, see the self-congratulatory account by Flick, 1 April 1940, NI-3345, RG238 M891/12/0165–92.

9. Ufermann, *Stahltrust*, 102.

10. Ibid., 3.

11. On the foundation of the VSt, see the excellent recent study by Alfred Reckendrees, *Das "Stahltrust"-Projekt: Die Gründung der Vereinigte Stahlwerke AG und ihre Unternehmensentwicklung 1926–1933/34* (München: Edition Hentrich, 2000).

12. Testimony of Flick, 2 July 1947, RG238 M891/5/0074.

13. See the discussion of the Gelsenkirchen deal in Turner, *German Big Business*, 254–59; Gerhard Volkland, "Hintergründe und politische Auswirkungen der Gelsenkirchen-Affäre im Jahre 1932," *Zeitschrift für Geschichtswissenschaft* 11 (1963), 289–318; most recently, Alfred Reckendrees and Kim Priemel, "Politik als produktive Kraft? Die 'Gelsenberg-Affäre' und die Krise des Flick-Konzerns (1931/32)," *Jahrbuch für Wirtschaftsgeschichte* (2006), 63–93; Henning Köhler, "Zum Verhältnis Friedrich Flicks zur Reichsregierung am Ende der Weimarer Republik," in *Industrielles System und politische Entwicklung in der Weimarer Republik*, ed. Hans Mommsen, Dietmar Petzina, and Bernd Weisbrod (Düsseldorf: Droste Verlag, 1974), 878–83.

14. Details about Flick's participation in German political life are sketchy. Henry Turner notes his support in 1924 for the National Liberal Union, a group com-

prising DVP followers disgruntled with Gustav Stresemann's willingness to traffic with the Social Democrats; aside from this, there is little else to suggest a strong preference for particular policy alternatives: Henry Ashby Turner Jr., *Stresemann and the Politics of the Weimar Republic* (Princeton: Princeton University Press, 1963), 158.

15. Turner, *German Big Business and the Rise of Hitler*, 258.

16. Affadavit of Wilhelm Keppler, NI-903, RG238 M891/15/0945–48.

17. See Reinhard Vogelsang, *Der Freundeskreis Himmler* (Göttingen: Musterschmidt, 1976), 32, 38–39, 62; on the significance of Flick and Steinbrinck's participation in Himmler's group, see the letter of Hitler to Himmler, 21 September 1943, EC-453, *Nazi Conspiracy and Aggression*, VII (Washington, DC: U.S. Government Printing Office, 1946), 510–12.

18. See especially Stallbaumer, "Strictly Business?"

19. Harold James, *The Deutsche Bank and the Nazi Economic War against the Jews: The Expropriation of Jewish-owned Property* (Cambridge: Cambridge University Press, 2001), 212–15; idem, "Die Deutsche Bank und die Diktatur 1933–1945," in *Die Deutsche Bank 1870–1945*, ed. Lothar Gall et al. (München: Verlag C. H. Beck, 1995), 344–51; on the bank expropriations generally, see Ingo Köhler, *Die "Arisierung" der Privatbanken im Dritten Reich: Verdrängung, Ausschaltung, und die Frage der Wiedergutmachung* (München: Verlag C. H. Beck, 2005).

20. Peter Hayes, "Big Business and 'Aryanization' in Germany, 1933–1939," *Jahrbuch für Antisemitismusforschung* 3 (1994), 265.

21. Memorandum of Steinbrinck to Flick, 6 October 1934, NI-5334, RG238 T301/156; Notiz Betr.: Simson/Suhl, 9 May 1935, NI-5335, RG238 M891/14/0232–33.

22. Notiz. Betr. Simson/Suhl, 9 May 1935, NI-5335, RG238 M891/14/0232–33.

23. Stallbaumer, "Strictly Business?," 126.

24. File note of Steinbrinck, 23 May 1935, NI-5336, RG238 T301/156.

25. See Notiz Betr.: Simson/Suhl, 23 May 1935, NI-5337, RG238 M891/14/0236–38, for the Flick concern's specific reservations regarding price, future labor questions, and provision of raw materials.

26. Helmut Genschel, *Die Verdrängung der Juden aus der Wirtschaft im Dritten Reich* (Göttingen: Musterschmidt, 1966), 102–3.

27. Erich Buchmann, *Von der jüdischen Firma Simson zur Nationalsozialistischer Industriestiftung Gustloff Werke*, Thüringer Untersuchungen zur Judenfrage 10 (Erfurt: U. Bodung, 1944), 16. Buchmann's account is a grossly anti-Semitic piece of propaganda.

28. Stallbaumer suggests the intriguing possibility that Flick sought to assist the state in countering party initiatives: "Strictly Business?," 130–31.

29. Mark Spoerer, *Von Scheingewinn zum Rüstungsboom: Die Eigenkapital-rentabilität der deutschen Industrieaktiengesellschaften 1925–1941* (Stuttgart: F. Steiner, 1996), 147. Using recently accessible archival material, Spoerer demonstrates that capital returns increased by more than 15 percent during the 1930s, tapering off slightly in 1941.

30. R. J. Overy, *The Nazi Economic Recovery 1932–1938*, 2nd ed. (Cambridge: Cambridge University Press, 1996), 52.

31. See especially Timothy Mason, *Social Policy in the Third Reich: The Working Class and the "National Community"* (Providence, Oxford: Berg, 1993), 106–7.

32. See the excellent essay, detailing what lay at stake for heavy industry and its mounting political impotence, by R. J. Overy, "Heavy Industry and the Third Reich: The Reichswerke Crisis," in idem, *War and Economy in the Third Reich* (Oxford: Oxford University Press, 1994), 93–118; also A. E. Simpson, "The Struggle for Control of the German Economy, 1936–37," *Journal of Modern History* 21 (1959), 37–45.

33. David Schoenbaum, *Hitler's Social Revolution: Class and Status in Nazi Germany 1933–1939* (New York/London: Norton, 1980), 116.

34. Peter Hayes, *Industry and Ideology: IG Farben in the Nazi Era* (Cambridge: Cambridge University Press, 1987), 177; idem, "Industrie und Ideologie: Die IG Farben in der Zeit des Nationalsozialismus," *Zeitschrift für Unternehmensgeschichte* 32 (1987), 132; divisions among IG's senior executives are described in idem, "Carl Bosch and Carl Krauch: Chemistry and the Political Economy of Germany 1925–1945," *Journal of Economic History* 47 (1987), 153–63.

35. Overy, "Heavy Industry and the Third Reich," 116.

36. The label "*stille Teilhaber*" comes from Avraham Barkai, "German Entrepreneurs and Jewish Policy in the Third Reich," *Yad Vashem Studies* 21 (1991), 126.

37. Genschel, *Verdrängung*, 222; see Verordnung zur Durchführung des Vierjahresplans, 18 October 1936, Bu-873, RG238 M891/31/0285; Zweite Verordnung zur Durchführung des Vierjahresplans, 5 November 1936, Bu-874, RG238 M891/31/0288; and extracts from the report on Göring's speech on the plan before leading industrialists at the "Preussenhaus," 17 December 1936: Über die Durchführung des Vierjahresplans, NI-051, RG238 M891/14/088–095.

38. Matthias Riedel, *Eisen und Kohle für das Dritte Reich: Paul Pleigers Stellung in der NS-Wirtschaft* (Göttingen: Musterschmidt, 1973), 32–33.

39. Testimony of Flick, 3 July 1947, RG238 M891/22/0855.

40. A recent account of the organization itself is Volker Ackermann, *Treffpunkt der Eliten: Die Geschichte des Industrie-Clubs Düsseldorf* (Düsseldorf: Droste, 2006).

41. Overy, "Heavy Industry and the Third Reich," 104–5.

42. Testimony of Flick, 3 July 1947, RG238 M891/22/0856–57.

43. Overy, "Heavy Industry and the Third Reich," 105.

44. Göring to Flick, 13 August 1937, NI-3488, RG238 M891/14/0833.

45. Stallbaumer, "Strictly Business?," 141–42.

46. The seven in question were Flick's, VSt, Krupp, Gutehoffnungshütte, Hoesch, Mannesmann, and Klöckner. See Dietrich Eichholtz, *Geschichte der deutschen Kriegswirtschaft 1939–1945*, vol. 1, *1939–1941* (Berlin: Akademie Verlag, 1984), 51.

47. Gerhard Thomas Mollin, "Der Strukturwandel der Montanindustrie in der NS-Wirtschaft," in *Der Zweite Weltkrieg: Analysen, Grundzüge, Forschungsbilanz*, ed. Wolfgang Michalka (Munich: Serie Piper, 1989), 367.

48. Peter Hayes, "Big Business and 'Aryanization,'" 267.

49. Genschel, *Verdrängung*, 218–19.

50. Stallbaumer, "Strictly Business?," 165–66.

51. Notiz. Betr.: Lübeck, 24 January 1935, NI-1843a, RG238 M891/14/0259–60.

52. Stallbaumer, "Strictly Business?," 168–69.

53. Genschel, *Verdrängung*, 222–23.

54. Niederschrift über die Besprechung vom 1.12.37 betr. Rawack & Grünfeld A.G., 1 December 1937, NI-2620, RG238 M891/14/0298–301.

55. Notiz. Heutige Besprechung mit Herrn Spiegelberg, 6 December 1937, NI-2625, RG238 M891/14/0307–12.

56. Ibid.

57. Ibid.; Letter of Spiegelberg to Flick, 9 December 1937, NI-4839, RG238 M891/14/0317–18.

58. Schreiben des Generalbevollmächtigten für Eisenwirtschaft an die Hahn'schen Werke, 10 December 1937, NI-2626, RG238 M891/14/0326.

59. Testimony of Defendent Flick, *TWC*, 604: "Our brown coal basis at Lauchhammer, that is in the Lausitz, was very feeble and very small. . . . As brown coal and brown coal briquettes were vital for the Mitteldeutsche Stahlwerke . . . we, of course, had an interest there to strengthen the basis of our plants as far as fuel was concerned and to prolong their life. . . . It is not a very comfortable situation for a plant if you have to think that after about 25 years you would be there without any raw material basis at all." Flick later estimated that the Julius and Ignaz Petschek "groups together control approximately one-third of German brown coal deposits." Untitled memorandum of Flick, 19 January 1938, NI-784, RG238 M891/14/0407–17.

60. Stallbaumer, "Strictly Business?," 219.

61. Testimony of Defendent Flick, *TWC*, 601, 604. Lignite, while suitable for power production at Flick's Mittelstahl plant, could not be used in the smelting of pig iron; the blast furnaces required a combination of soft coal and coke.

62. Notiz. Betr.: Petschek-Frage—Rücksprache mit Herbert Göring am 23.12, 23 December 1937, St-57, RG238 M891/31/1231.

63. Göring to Flick, 21 January 1938, NI-900, RG238 M891/14/0497.

64. Stallbaumer, "Strictly Business?," 223.

65. Aktenvermerk. Betr.: Petschek-Komplex. Mitteilung von Herbert Göring am 5.1, 5 January 1938, NI-3252, RG238 M891/14/0445–46.

66. Untitled memorandum of Flick, 19 January 1938, NI-784, RG238 M891/14/0407–17. The authorization to conduct negotiations alone or on behalf of a consortium of interests is contained in Göring to Flick, 21 January 1938, NI-900, RG238 M891/14/0497; reaffirmed in Göring to Flick, 1 February 1938, NI-899, RG238 M891/14/0530.

67. For a detailed account of the negotiations between Flick and Murnane, see Stallbaumer, "Strictly Business?," 231–37.

68. Notiz Betr.: Petschek Angelegenheit, 17 February 1938, NI-3241, RG238 M891/14/0547. Steinbrinck's comments point out that some officials, notably Keppler and Pleiger, favored some form of direct intervention. After the *Anschluß* of Austria on 12–13 March 1938, relations between the United States and Nazi Germany worsened, which likely contributed to a willingness to take stronger measures. Treading a fine line, Steinbrinck advised that the Flick concern discourage political involvement out of fear that the Four-Year Plan organization could nationalize the assets.

69. Ibid.

70. File note of Flick, 24.5.1938, NI-5524, *TWC*, 472–74; the question of price is discussed in Memorandum of Steinbrinck, 21.2.1938, St-366a, *TWC*, 468; the requisite foreign exchange was provided by Wintershall: Notiz. Betr.: Petschek Angelegenheit, 17 February 1938, NI-3241, RG238 M891/14/0547.

71. Stallbaumer, "Strictly Business?," 244–45; Letter from Körner to Flick, 25.5.1938, NI-3320, *TWC*, 475–76.

72. File note of Flick, 24.5.1938, NI-5524, *TWC*, 472–74; Anlage IV, 10 January 1938, NI-3254, RG238 M891/14/0466–69.

73. Anlage IV, 10 January 1938, NI-3254, RG238 M891/14/0466–69.

74. Aktenvermerk. Betr.: Ignaz Petschek.—Unterredung mit Ministerialdirektor Wohltat am 4.10, 5 October 1938, NI-3314, RG238 M891/14/0678–80; Aktenvermerk. Betr.: Ignaz Petschek. Unterredung mit Staatsrat Reinhart am 21.2, 22 December 1938, RG238 M891/31/1224–25.

75. Problem Ignaz Petschek, 20 June 1938, NI-896, RG238 M891/14/0650–56.

76. Stallbaumer, "Strictly Business?," 272–75.

77. Aktennotiz. Betr.: Ignaz Petschek, 13 October 1938 NI-894, RG238 M891/14/0687–88.

78. Decree concerning the use of Jewish property, 3 December 1938, PS-1409, *TWC*, 498–503.

79. Stallbaumer does not believe that Flick actually expected to be awarded the trusteeship at this juncture: "Strictly Business?," 286, note 64; the source is Aktenvermerk. Betr.: Ignaz Petschek—Unterredung mit Bergrat Gabel am 14.1, 14 January 1939, NI-3290, RG238 M891/14/0710–15.

80. Aktenvermerk. Betr.: Ignaz Petschek—Unterredung mit Bergrat Gabel am 14.1, 14 January 1939, NI-3290, RG238 M891/14/0710–15.

81. Aktennotiz. Betr.: Problem I. P.—Unterredung mit Dr. Voss am 2.2, 2 February 1939, NI-889, RG238 M891/14/0727–32.

82. Austausch von Steinkohle gegen Braunkohle, 9 December 1939, NI-937, RG238 M891/14/0875–83.

83. Stallbaumer, "Strictly Business?," 352ff, discusses in detail the contentious issues surrounding the final arrangement.

Chapter 3. The German Steel Industry before the Assimilation of Lorraine and Plans for Expropriation

1. Best on this broad subject remains Hans-Erich Volkmann, "Zur europäischen Dimesion nationalsozialistischer Wirtschaftspolitik," in *Ökonomie und Expansion: Grundzüge der NS-Wirtschaftspolitik. Ausgewählte Schriften von Hans-Erich Volkmann*, ed. Bernhard Chiari (München: R. Oldenbourg, 2003), 19–44.

2. Hermann Wedding, "Die Eisenerzvorräte Deutschlands," *Verhandlungen des Vereins zur Beförderung des Gewerbfleißes* 86 (1907), 198, 209.

3. Bähr et al., *Flick-Konzern*, 439; Reckendrees, *"Stahltrust"-Projekt*, 87ff.

4. Martin Fritz, *German Steel and Swedish Iron Ore, 1939–1945* (Göteborg: Institute of Economic History of Gothenburg University, 1974), 40.

5. See the reports by Max Scring, "Auswertung der Erfahrungen des Weltkrieges für die deutsche Heeres—und Volkswirtschaft der Gegenwart unter besonderer Berücksichtigung von Eisen und Nährung," October 1939, RG242 T71/20/411489; and OKW WiRüAmt, "Einfluß wirtschaftlicher Gesichtspunkte auf militärische Operationen," RG242 T71/92/595894. On the risks to the iron-ore supply of a blockade, see WStb, No. 7430/39 g.Kdos. Via Az. 3i/60/24, 25 August 1939, Nachrichtenblatt Wehrwirtschaft U.d.S.S.R. No. 1, BA-MA Wi/ID 19.

6. Wilhelm Treue, "Hitlers Denkschrift zum Vierjahresplan 1936," *Vierteljahreshefte für Zeitgeschichte* 3 (1955), 209; a highly partial contemporary treatment is by Paul Rheinländer, *Die deutsche Eisen- und Stahlwirtschaft im Vierjahresplan* (Berlin: Junker und Dunnhaupt, 1939); the standard work of the Four-Year Plan remains Dietmar Petzina, *Autarkiepolitik im Dritten Reich: Der nationalsozialistische Vierjahresplan* (Stuttgart: Deutsche Verlagsanstalt, 1968).

7. Jäger, *Wirtschaftliche Abhängigkeit*, 131; on the implications of the *Anschluß* for war production especially, see "Die wehrwirtschaftliche Bedeutung der Eingliederung Österreichs in den deutschen Wirtschaftsraum," RG242 T71/102/603975; also Norbert Schausberger, "Wirtschaftliche Aspekte des Anschlusses Österreichs an das Deutsche Reich: Ein Dokumentation," *Militärgeschichtliche Mitteilungen* 8 (1970).

8. See the discussion in Fritz, *German Steel and Swedish Iron Ore*, 88–89; Jäger estimates a savings in coke of 2 to 3 percent for each single percentage increase in iron content in the ore; *Wirtschaftliche Abhängigkeit*, 76. On the alarming shortage of skilled labor, see Reichswirtchaftsministerium, Hauptring Eisenerzeugung, Tätigkeitsberichte, RG242 T71/34/428355.

9. Institut für Weltwirtschaft, "Die Eisenerzversorgung Grossdeutschlands während der gegenwärtigen kriegerischen Verwicklungen," December 1939, RG242 T84/195/1560527.

10. Fritz, *German Steel and Swedish Iron Ore*, 23ff.

11. Speech of Schacht before the Economic Council, 29 November 1938, EC-611, *Nazi Conspiracy and Aggression*, vol. 7, 589ff.

12. Wirtschaftsgruppe Eisenschaffende Industrie, Eisen- und Stahlfragen— Besprechung mit Herrn General von Hanneken, 1938, R13 1/692, 105.

13. On this point, see particularly the survey by Rolf-Dieter Müller, "The Mobilization of the German Economy for Hitler's War Aims," in Rolf-Dieter Müller, Bernhard Kroener, and Hans Umbreit, *Germany and the Second World War*, vol. V/I, *Organization and Mobilization of the German Sphere of Power* (Oxford: Oxford University Press, 2000), 405–786; also Burton H. Klein, *Germany's Economic Preparations for War* (Cambridge: Harvard University Press, 1959), 114–35; B. A. Carroll, *Design for Total War: Arms and Economics in the Third Reich* (The Hague, Paris: Mouton, 1968).

14. Petzina, *Autarkiepolitik*, 103; see the discussion in Fritz, *German Steel and Swedish Iron Ore*, 21–23.

15. Hans-Erich Volkmann, "Aussenhandel und Aufrüstung in Deutschland, 1933 bis 1939," in *Wirtschaft und Rüstung am Vorabend des Zweiten Weltkrieges*, ed. Friedrich Forstmeier and Hans-Erich Volkmann (Düsseldorf: Droste, 1975), 85–89.

16. Reichstelle für Wirtschaftsausbau, "Sofortmaßnahmen im Mob-Fall auf Grund der heutigen Versorgungslage auf den Rohstoffgebieten," 18 October 1938, NI-8837, T-71/108/611495.

17. Germany absorbed 70 to 75 percent of Swedish ore exports; the remainder flowed to Britain and the United States: Aktennotiz des Wehrwirtschafts- und Rüstungsamtes des OKW über die Besprechung am 18. Dezember 1939, *Anatomie des Krieges*, 236.

18. On this point, long acknowledged, see the exchanges between Rolf Karlbom and Jörg-Johannes Jäger in the *The Scandanavian Economic Review*, nos. 13 (1965); 15 (1967); and 16 (1968). Also A. S. Milward, "Could Sweden Have Stopped the Second World War?," *The Scandanavian Economic Review* 15 (1967), 127.

19. Alan Milward, *The New Order and the French Economy* (Oxford: Oxford University Press, 1970), 212.

20. Aktennotiz Betr: Besprechung bei Generalfeldmarschall Göring in Karinhall am 30.1.1940, EC-606, RG238 M891/14/1059; also in *Nazi Conspiracy and Aggression*, vol. 7, 588.

21. On the strategic vulnerability of the German economy from a military perspective, see Murray, *Change in the European Balance of Power*, 8–9.

22. Figures cited in Mollin, *Montankonzerne und Drittes Reich*, 222.

23. Proposals by Leiter der Wigru Metallindustrie re: Großraumwirtschaft, 15 August 1940, RG242 T71/8/400660.

24. Good visual perspectives on the region, including the ore reserves and steel mill in it, can be found in Société d'éditions géographiques professionelles, *Fonderies de fonte et d'acier* (Paris, 1971); and Armelle Rousseau, *De fonte et d'acier* (Thionville: G. Klopp, 1995).

25. As a result of its low iron content, ore from Lorraine was referred to as "minette."

26. See the study by Markus Nievelstein, *Der Zug nach der Minette: Deutsche Unternehmen in Lothringen, 1871–1918. Handlungsspielräume und Strategien im Spannungsfeld des deutsch-französisichen Grenzgebietes* (Bochum: N. Brockmeyer, 1993).

27. Strukturveränderungern der deutschen Wirtschaft, insbesondere der Ruhrindustrie, im Zusammenhang mit der Abtretung Lothringens und dem Ausscheiden sowohl des Saargebietes als auch Luxemburgs aus dem deutschen Zollgebiet, March 1927, BA R131/287, 4.

28. Wilfried Feldenkirchen, *Die Eisen- und Stahlindustrie des Ruhrgebiets 1879–1914. Wachstum, Finanzierung und Unternehmensstruktur ihrer Großunternehmen*, Beiheft 20, *Zeitschrift für Unternehmensgeschichte* (Wiesbaden: Steiner, 1982), 61, n. 18; Diether Döring, *Die deutschen Schwerindustriellen Interessen in Lothringen bis 1914* (Frankfurt am Main, 1971), 123.

29. The key deposits extended south from the borders of Belgium and Luxemburg approximately 60 kilometers along the west bank of the Moselle River as far as Nancy. Around Thionville-Briey they attain a width of some 30 kilometers; see the column by Paul Raabe, "Das Lothringische Minette-Gebiet und seine wirtschaftliche Bedeutung," *Stahl und Eisen* 61/2 (9 January 1941), 45–46.

30. *German Designs on French Lorraine: The Secret Memorandum of the German Iron and Steel Manufacturers* (London: G. Allen and Unwin, 1918), 17–18ff. See also the contemporary emphasis on Lorraine's strategic importance in F. Beyschlag and P. Krusch, *Deutschlands künftige Versorgung mit Eisen- und Mangenerzen: Eine lagerstättenkundliche Gutachten im Auftrage des Vereins deutscher Eisen- und Stahlindustrieller und des Vereins deutscher Eisenhüttenleute* (Berlin, 1917).

31. On the basic orientation of the German steel industry in that period, see Stefanie van de Kerkhof, *Von der Friedens- zur Kriegswirtschaft: Unternehmenstrategien der deutschen Eisen- und Stahlindustrie vom Kaiserreich bis zum Ende des Ersten Weltkrieges* (Essen: Klartext, 2006).

32. Auszüge aus einer Ausarbeitung von Professor Sering über "Auswertung der Erfahrungen des Weltkrieges für die deutsche Heeres- und Volkswirtschaft der Gegenwart unter besonderer Berücksichtigung von Eisen und Nahrung," 15 January 1940, BA RW19/567.

33. Aktenvermerk des Oberkommandos der Kriegsmarine, "Eisen und Kohle im neuen deutschen Machtbereich, die Grundlage für die zukünftige deutsche Eisenindustrie," 27 June 1940, BA R13I/673; also in Eichholtz, *Geschichte der deutschen Kriegswirtschaft*, 295–98.

34. Expert testimony of Wenzel in September 1927: *Zur Frage der Eisenerzversorgung Deutschlands, insbesondere Rheinland-Westfalens*, in *Die Rohstoffversorgung der deutschen eisenerzeugenden Industrie. Verhandlungen und Berichte des Unterausschusses für Gewerbe: Industrie, Handel und Handwerk*, ed. Ausschuß zur Untersuchung der Erzeugungs- und Absatzbedingungen der deutschen Wirtschaft, III, *Unterausschuß* (Berlin: E. S. Mittler und Sohn, 1928), 55.

35. See the report by J. W. Reichert, "Frankreichs Eisenpolitik," *Der deutsche Volkswirt*, 14. Jahrgang, No. 40, 5 July 1940, 140, BA R13 I/616, 161.

36. Wilhelm Treue and Helmut Uebbing, *Die feuer verlöschen nie: August Thyssen-Hütte 1926–1966* (Düsseldorf, Wien: Econ Verlag, 1966), 231ff.

37. Cited in Rainer Haus, *Lothringen und Salzgitter in der Eisenerzpolitik der deutschen Schwerindustrie von 1871–1940*, ed. Archiv der Stadt Salzgitter, *Salzgitter Forschungen*, vol. 1 (Salzgitter: Archiv der Stadt Salzgitter, 1991), 255; by 1940, the "Memorandum Schoen," as it was called, was seen by wary officials as underpinning hasty and excessive demands for annexations by industrial concerns: see Schreiben von Ernst Poensgen an die Mitglieder des "Kleinen Kreises" vom 27. Juni 1940, in Eichholtz, *Geschichte der deutschen Kriegswirtschaft*, 298–301.

38. Haus, *Lothringen und Salzgitter*, 258.

39. Testimony of Steinbrinck, 1 August 1947, RG238 M891/24/0236; Testimony of Hanneken, 23 July 1947, RG238 M891/6/0022.

40. Protokoll von Erich Tgahrt über die Besprechung im "Kleinen Kreis," 7 June 1940, Eichholtz, *Geschichte der deutschen Kriegswirtschaft*, 295.

41. Verteilungsvorschläge der Reichstelle für Eisen und Stahl für die luxemburgische und frans.-lothringische Eisenindustrie, Berlin, 26 July 1940, NI-3518, RG238 M891/14/1185, 4.

42. Deposition of Paul Raabe, 11 September 1945, PS-2217, RG238 M891/14/1106.

43. Testimony of Hans Hahl, RG238 M891/18/0770 and RG238 M891/14/1112–21.

44. Testimony of Steinbrinck, RG238 M891/24/0237–38.

45. Hermann Röchling, "Lothringens Eisenindustrie," *Stahl und Eisen* 61/2 (9 January 1941), 46–47.

46. Beauftragter für den Vierjahresplan, V.P. 11964/5 vom 2.8.1940, EC-137, Betr.: Deutscher Einfluß bei ausländischen Unternehmen, RG238 M891/14/1029–32.

47. Deposition of Paul Raabe, 11 September 1945, PS-2217, RG238 M891/14/1103.

48. Testimony of Kranzbühler, 23 July 1947, RG238 M891/6/0037.

49. Letter of Poensgen, Protokoll der Sitzung des Kleinen Kreises vom 7.6.1940, BA R13I/621; also NI-048, RG238 M891/14/1144–52; also in Thieleke, *Fall 5*, 215–19; an account of the same is provided by the chairman of the board of Hoesch AG, Erich Tgahrt, in Eichholtz, *Geschichte der Kriegswirtschaft*, 294–95.

50. Overy, *Goering*, 124.

51. Aktennotiz von Alfred Brüninghaus vom 17. Juli 1940, in Eichholtz, *Geschichte der deutschen Kriegswirtschaft*, 312. The file note references a conference held with Poensgen on the previous day.

52. Hanneken indicated as much to Poensgen in conversation: "Herr von Hanneken confirms that such views are present in government offices"; Schreiben von Ernst Poensgen an die Mitglieder des "Kleinen Kreises" vom 27. Juni 1940, Eichholtz, *Geschichte der deutschen Kriegswirtschaft*, 299.

53. Aktenvermerk über die Besprechung im Hauptquartier des Generalfeldmarschall Göring v.19.6.1940, PS-1155, RG238 M891/14/1025 and RG238 M891/18/0717.

54. Letter of Poensgen, Protokoll der Sitzung des Kleinen Kreises vom 7.6.1940, BA R13I/621; also NI-048, RG238 M891/14/1144–52; also in Thieleke, *Fall 5*, 215–19; an account of the same is provided by the chairman of the board of Hoesch AG, Erich Tgahrt, in Eichholtz, *Geschichte der deutschen Kriegswirtschaft*, 294–95.

55. A notable exception was Flick, who refused to endorse this position, presumably for reasons reflected in objections he raised during the meeting of the Small Circle detailed above. Flick asserted that the earlier dispossession of

property in Upper Silesia should factor into decisions regarding the distribution of expropriated property in the West: Testimony of Flick, 22 May 1947, RG238 M891/4/0039–40.

56. Letter of Rombacher Hüttenwerke to the civil administrator, Betr: Antrag auf Feldesbegehren, 9 March 1942, RG242 T83/55/3423871–5, gives a brief history of the French expropriation campaign in Lorraine after World War I and Germany's legal position in 1940.

57. Testimony of Flick, 10 July 1947, RG238 M891/5/0408–9.

58. Schreiben von Ernst Poensgen an die Mitglieder des "Kleinen Kreises" vom 27. Juni 1940, Eichholtz, *Geschichte der deutschen Kriegswirtschaft*, 299.

59. Testimony of Hermann Röchling, 15 September 1947, RG238 M891/1/324; Hans Hahl, manager of the Rodinger works, indicated that Röchling also lost the Diedenhofen steel plant, but no mention is made in the sources of compensation for the latter: Testimony of Hans Hahl, RG238 M891/18/0767.

60. Notiz Burkart—Betr: Besprechung mit Herrn von Hanneken am 10. Juni, 11 June 1940, NI-3516, RG238 M891/14/1155–58; see also Hanneken's treatment of the issue in postwar trial proceedings, RG238 M891/21/0729.

61. See the earlier discussion between Hanneken and the leading figures of the steel industry, including Flick, Krupp, Klöckner, Vögler, Reichert, and Poensgen: Wirtschaftsgruppe Eisenschaffende Industrie, Eisen und Stahlfragen— Besprechung mit Herrn General von Hanneken, BA R13I/692, 105.

62. Rundschreiben der Wirtschaftsgruppe Eisenschaffende Industrie, 26 June 1940, NI-3526, Thieleke, *Fall 5*, 220–22.

63. Aktenvermerk des Oberkommandos der Kriegsmarine, "Eisen und Kohle im neuen deutschen Machtbereich, die Grundlage für die zukünftige deutsche Eisenindustrie," 27 June 1940, BA R13I/1004; also in Eichholtz, *Geschichte der deutschen Kriegswirtschaft*, 295–98.

64. Vertrauliche Darstellung der Wirtschaftsgruppe Eisenschaffende Industrie, "Die Bedeutung der lothringische-luxemburgischen Erzbecken," 25 June 1940, RG242 T71/135/633086; also BA R13I/1095.

65. Notiz Burkart—Betr: Besprechung mit Herrn von Hanneken am 10. Juni, 11 June 1940, NI-3516, RG238 M891/14/1155–58.

66. Flick to Buskühl, 23 June 1940, NI-3513, RG238 M891/14/1132–36.

67. Deposition of Hans Hahl (assistant director of the Foreign Department "South West" of the Reich Iron Association), 11 September 1945, RG238 M891/14/1114–15.

68. See Gerhard Seibold, *Röchling: Kontinuität im Wandel* (Suttgart: Jan Thorbecke, 2001).

69. See Röchling's strident interwar revisionist tract on the question, published by the so-called Volk und Reich Verlag: Hermann Röchling, *Wir Halten die Saar!* (Berlin: Volk und Reich Verlag, 1934).

70. See Bruno Rauecker, *Die sozialen und wirtschaftlichen Beziehungen zwischen Elsass-Lothringen und dem Saargebiet, 1920–1945* (Heidelberg: K. Vowinckel, 1937).

71. Mollin, *Montankonzerne und "Drittes Reich,"* 71–72.

72. Memorandum on the Commissioner General for Iron and Steel Production, II L Nr.2722/40, 1 July 1940, NI-3751, RG238 M891/18/0734 and RG238 M891/14/1063.

73. Burkart to Schrieker, 24 June 1940, NI-3525, RG238 M891/14/1134.

74. Notiz für Flick, 24 June 1940, NI-3525, RG238 M891/14/1135; Notiz für Flick, 26 June 1940, NI-3540, RG238 M891/14/1138; Notiz für Flick, 2 July 1940, NI-3519, RG238 M891/14/1141.

75. Anordnung zur Sicherstellung des planmässigen Ausbaues der Eisenindustrie in Lothringen, No. 630, *Verordnungsblatt für Lothringen* (1941), 1006.

76. On the substance of Röchling's report, withheld from other members of the steel industry but shared with Reichert, see the comments of Fritz von Bruck, then the director of Hoesch and head of the company's Berlin branch office: Aktennotiz von Fritz von Bruck vom 7. Juli 1940, Eichholtz, *Geschichte der deutschen Kriegswirtschaft*, 301–2.

77. Burkart Notiz für Flick, 4 July 1940, NI-3522, RG238 M891/14/1178–79; Poensgen specifically solicits Flick's advice, asks whether the latter has designs on any plants in the near west, and promises to do nothing without first consulting Flick.

Chapter 4. Friedrich Flick's Campaign to Acquire the Rombach Works, 1940–1944

1. On Flick's expansion into occupied French territories, see Kim C. Priemel, *Flick. Eine Konzerngeschichte vom Kaiserreich bis zur Bundesrepublik* (Göttingen: Wallstein, 2007), 438ff.

2. See the excellent discussion of this issue in Peter Hayes, "Polycracy and Policy in the Third Reich: The Case of the Economy," in *Reevaluating the Third Reich*, ed. Thomas Childers and Jane Caplan (New York: Holmes and Meier, 1993).

3. See R. J. Overy, *Goering: "The Iron Man"* (London: Routledge and Kegan Paul, 1984), 15–16.

4. Bericht—vorgenommene Prüfung der wirtschaftlichen und steuerlichen Verhältnisse bei der Rombacher Hüttenwerke, 29 August 1941, RG242 T83/55/3423888–910. The Machern works were apparently in very poor condition in 1940; two of the four furnaces at Machern were considered "ripe for demolition," leading an official assessment to rate them at 10 percent of their nominal value: "Aufgabe und Zusammensetzung der Kommission," 21 February 1941, NI-5487, RG238 M891/14/1283–1304.

5. That Flick considered his prospects for acquiring the Rombach plant favorable had partly to do with the fortunes of the plant's pre-1918 owners, the Später family, which by 1940 had declined to such an extent that they could not resume control of their former assets: Testimony of Flick, 10 July 1947, RG238 M891/23/0045; Testimony of Hans Hahl, 8 July 1947, RG238 M891/14/1113.

6. Jacques Laurent, the manager of the works in 1940, listed the principal firms involved in establishing Rombach as Société Aciéries de la Marine et d'Homecourt and Aciéries de Micheville; French Affadavit of Jacques Laurent, NI-5396, RG238 M891/14/1125–31.

7. Due to the complete absence of open-cast mining, the cost of extracting the ore in the southern reaches of the Lorraine minette belt was much higher than in Luxemburg and Longwy. Experts calculated an extraction price of RM 4–4.5 per ton of ore for Rombach, nearly twice the cost of extracting ore in the north: Notiz Betr.: Lothringen-Luxemburg, 16 August 1940, NI-3539, RG238 M891/14/1211.

8. "Aufgabe und Zusammensetzung der Kommission," 21 February 1941, NI-5487, RG238 M891/14/1283–1304.

9. This number probably includes the capacity of the Homecourt plant as well, which belonged to the same industrial group as Rombach. According to Flick's associate, statistics from the period between 1920 and 1940 revealed a maximum capacity of 678,000 tons of steel for Rombach and 300,000 to 350,000 tons for Homecourt: Testimony of Odilo Burkart, 4 September 1947, RG238 M891/25/0748; also RG238 M891/21/0706.

10. Chief among these shareholdings were the Société des Ciments Portland de Rombas (Mosel), Société des Constructions Metaliques de la Vallée de l'Orne à Mézières- les Metz (Mosel), Charbonnages de Faulquemont (Mosel), Société des Mines d'Anderny-Chevillon (Meurthe u. Mosel). There is no indication that Flick's acquisition of Rombach brought with it influence over the foregoing firms.

11. Flick's technical experts estimated the cost of importing coke to the occupied West at RM 8 per ton, regardless of whether the destination lay in the northern or southern reaches of the minette basin. Completion of a canal from the Mosel River would have lowered the cost of transporting coke to the south by RM 1–2 per ton: Notiz Betr.: Lothringen-Luxemburg, 16 August 1940, NI-3539, RG238 M891/14/1212.

12. Hugo Klein was director and chairman of the board of the Siegener Hütte when appointed to head the ministerial commission: "Aufgabe und Zusammensetzung der Kommission," 21 February 1941, NI-5487, RG238 M891/14/1283.

13. Notiz für Herrn Dr. Flick, Betr: Rombach/Betriebsüberlassungsvertrag/ Steuerfragen, 18 August 1943, RG242 T83/55/3423742–43.

14. Richtlinien des Generalbeauftragten für Eisen und Stahl in Lothringen und Meurthe-et-Moselle, 5 July 1940, Bu-819, RG238 M891/31/0096.

15. Flick listed the German firms to which the major plants in Lorraine would go. VSt would receive Differdingen, Klöckner would receive Kneuttingen, Röchling would receive Carlshütte bei Diedenhofen, Stumm would receive Ueckingen, and Dillinger would receive Redingen. Flick had heard rumors that the Reichswerke would acquire the large holdings of the de Wendel family, including its massive coal deposits in Germany, Lorraine, and Holland, as well as Hagendingen (the last by virtue of being the successor firm to Thyssen): Memorandum from Flick to Buskühl, 23 June 1940, NI-3513, RG238 M891/14/1161–67.

16. BA-MA RW35/858, 6 January 1941, Bericht an den Oberbefehlshaber des Heeres Herrn Generalfeldmarschall von Brauchitsch—Kohlenversorgung. The report advised a major revision of supply guidelines to guard against a production decrease damaging to the war economy. Matters were not helped by a massive strike in Belgium soon thereafter over the poor food-supply situation, which placed at risk 26 percent of the Reich's coal supply: Wolfram Weber, *Die innere Sicherheit im besetzten Belgien und Nordfrankreich 1940–1944: Ein Beitrag zur Geschichte der Besatzungsverwaltungen* (Düsseldorf: Droste Verlag, 1978), 55–56.

17. Memorandum from Flick to Buskühl, 23 June 1940, NI-3513, RG238 M891/14/1161–67; see also 22-May-DJG-11–4-Ninabuck (Schlesinger), RG238 M891/4/0047.

18. Memorandum from Flick to Buskühl, 23 June 1940, NI-3513, RG238 M891/14/1161–67.

19. Ibid.

20. Testimony of Flick, 10 July 1947, RG238 M891/23/0044–45.

21. Testimony of Flick, 10 July 1947, RG238 M891/23/0046–47.

22. Ibid.

23. The description comes from a statement that Hanneken gave after the war: Affidavit of Hermann von Hanneken, 22 April 1947, NI-6019, RG238 M891/14/0365.

24. Notiz Betr.: Besprechung mit Herrn von Hanneken am 10. Juni, 11 June 1940, NI-3516, RG238 M891/14/1155–58.

25. Reichert of WigruEisen, "Wünsche für den Friedensvertrag und die Neugestaltung der europäischen Wirtschaftsbeziehungen," 26 June 1940, NI-3526, RG238 M891/14/1170–71.

26. Karl Raabe to Flick, 2 July 1940, NI-3531, RG238 M891/14/1174.

27. Ibid.; see also Raabe's presentation before a high-level conference involving the key officials of the concern in August: Notiz Betr.: Lothringen-Luxemburg, 16 August 1940, NI-3539, RG238 M891/14/1211–16.

28. Burkart to Flick, Betr.: Lothringen/Aussprache im Kleinen Kreis, 4 July 1940, NI-3522, RG238 M891/14/1178–79.

29. Verteilungsvorschläge der Reichstelle für Eisen und Stahl für die luxemburgische und frans.-lothringische Eisenindustrie, Berlin, 26 July 1940, NI-3518, RG238 M891/14/1181–1202.

30. A smelting operation required an average of 1.52 tons of coking coal per ton of pig iron produced; with 2.7, Flick held the largest reserve surplus of coal per ton of potential iron output by a wide margin. By way of comparison, the ratios given by the report for the other major producers were Hoesch with 2.08, Mannesmann with 1.72, VSt with 1.3, and Klöckner with 1.24. Krupp, Gutehoffnungshütte, and the Reichswerke approximated the bare average required. These ratios do not reflect Flick's substantial brown-coal deposits, which were unsuitable for the purposes of coking: 22 May 47-A-SW-14-7-Fitzgerald (Hildesheimer), RG238 M891/4/0060.

31. Verteilungsvorschläge der Reichstelle für Eisen und Stahl für die luxemburgische und frans.-lothringische Eisenindustrie, Berlin, 26 July 1940, NI-3518, RG238 M891/14/1186.

32. Verteilungsvorschläge der Reichstelle für Eisen und Stahl für die luxemburgische und frans.-lothringische Eisenindustrie, Berlin, 26 July 1940, NI-3518, RG238 M891/14/1189, 8. The report included a useful comparative breakdown of the targeted works and their likely German expropriators, as well as a map detailing their geographic position in the minette basin.

33. Weiss Notiz für Herrn Burkart, 5 August 1940, NI-3533, RG238 M891/14/1208.

34. Notiz Betr.: Lothringen-Luxemburg, 16 August 1940, NI-3539, RG238 M891/14/1211–16.

35. Ibid.

36. Memo: Rücksprache Vögler, 29 July 1940, NI-1991, RG238 M891/14/1205.

37. Rücksprache mit Herrn von Hanneken am 27 August 1940, NI-3529, RG238 M891/14/1219–20.

38. Kaletsch Notiz für Herrn Flick, 2 October 1940, NI-3542, RG238 M891/14/1223–34.

39. Flick to Poensgen, Betr.: Lothringen, Zuteilung von Erzgruben und Hüttenwerken, 2 October 1940, NI-2505, RG238 M891/14/1227–30.

40. Flick to Hanneken, Betr.: Lothringische Hüttenwerke, 7 October 1940, NI-2506, RG238 M891/14/1233–37.

41. Ibid.

42. Flick to Hanneken, Betr.: Lothringische Hüttenwerke, 7 October 1940, NI-2506, RG238 M891/14/1237, 5.

43. Flick to Göring, 1 November 1940, NI-3530, RG238 M891/14/1240. As Flick was apparently midway through an inspection tour of steel mills in Lorraine and Luxemburg, including Rombach and Homecourt, on 1 November (the

first such since Göring's ban on the travel of industrialists to the area), one may presume that an assistant dispatched the letter: Reise—Programm, 24 October 1940, NI-4976, RG238 M891/14/1252.

44. Betrifft: Lothringische Eisenindustrie, 1 November 1940, NI-3548, RG238 M891/14/1243–44. See also Flick's note to Körner, through whom the letter to Göring was apparently sent: Flick to Körner, 2 November 1940, NI-3528, RG238 M891/14/1247.

45. Affadavit of Hermann von Hanneken, NI-6019, 23 April 1947, RG238 M891/14/0364–68. It seems clear that much transpired that went undocumented in the months leading up to Göring's decision to cement Flick's prospects.

46. BA R3101/32262, 22 January 1941, Verteilung des Hüttenbesitzes in Lothringen und Luxemburg: Schreiben Hermann Röchlings an General von Hanneken 22.1.1941; also Abschrift, 22 January 1941, NI-3018, RG238 M891/12/0204–9.

47. On 27 May 1942, with the establishment of the *Reichsvereinigung Eisen* and his appointment as one of its three chairman (along with Walter Rohland and Alfried Krupp von Bohlen und Halbach), Röchling appointed Flick, who was one of seven members of the presidium, to manage the entire Central European Group of the organization. When this administrative arrangement fell through, he assigned substantial authority to the Main Ring of the Iron Producing Industry and cited Flick specifically as having accomplished a great deal in the "field of scrap iron, of which he had probably more experience than anyone else in Germany": Affadavit of Röchling, NI-5549, RG238 M891/17/1006.

48. Zuteilung Lothringer und Luxemburger Hüttenwerke (Einrichtung von Treuhänderschaften), 5 February 1941, NI-049, RG238 M891/14/0255–58. The memorandum provides a complete listing of the twenty-one works in Lorraine and Luxemburg and the trustees to whom they were handed over; see also Betr.: Eisenhütten in Lothringen, 31 January 1941, RG242 T83/55/3423715.

49. Schiettinger to Flick, 20 February 1941, NI-2508, RG238 M891/14/1262–63.

50. Affadavit of Hermann von Hanneken, NI-6019, 23 April 1947, RG238 M891/14/0364–68.

51. Deposition of Hans Hahl, 11 September 1945 RG238 M891/14/1112–21.

52. Flick to Bürckel, 1 March 1941, NI-1644, RG238 M891/14/1264–69. Copies of this statement were also sent to Kaletsch, Weiss, the governing board of Harpen, and the management of Rombach.

53. Betr.: Rombacher Hüttenwerke, 26 February 1941, NI-1764, RG238 M891/14/1271–73.

54. Abschrift, 1 March 1941, NI-2507, RG238 M891/14/1276–79. Karl Raabe, whom Flick detailed to Rombach from his Maxhütte plant, represented the concern in the transfer.

55. "Aufgabe und Zusammensetzung der Kommission," 21 February 1941, NI-5487, RG238 M891/14/1283–1304.

56. Betr.: Vertrag Luxemburg/Lothringen, 7 May 1941, NI-1651, RG238 M891/14/1307–11.

57. The preliminary drafts at issue are not available.

58. Zuteilung Lothringer und Luxemburger Hüttenwerke (Einrichtung von Treuhänderschaften), 5 February 1941, NI-049, RG238 M891/14/0255–58.

59. Notiz über die heutige Besprechung in Berlin, 27 May 1941, NI-1187, RG238 M891/14/1314–21.

60. Ibid.

61. Niederschrift über die Besprechung beim Chef der Zivilverwaltung für Lothringen in Saarbrücken, 5 June 1941, NI-2502, RG238 M891/15/0002–5.

62. Betr.: Überlassungsverträge für die lothringer Eisenhütten, 30 July 1941, NI-1888, RG238 M891/15/0008–11.

63. Ibid.

64. Ibid.

65. Reich Marshal of the German Reich, plenipotentiary for the Four-Year Plan, VP 12028, order of 27 July 1941, BA-MA RW31/11; quoted in Rolf-Dieter Müller, "The Failure of the Economic 'Blitzkrieg Strategy,'" in *Germany and the Second World War*, vol. IV, *The Attack on the Soviet Union*, ed. H. Boog, J. Förster, J. Hoffmann, E. Klink, R.-D. Müller, and G. Ueberschär (Oxford: Oxford University Press, 1998), 1089.

66. Aktennotiz von Odilo Burkart für Flick, 13 August 1941, NI-5262, in Eichholtz and Schumann, *Anatomie des Krieges*, 348–49; also Schreiben von Hermann Göring an den Wirtschaftsführungsstab Ost, 2 November 1942, ibid., 216.

67. Betriebsüberlassungsvertrag, 15 December 1942, NI-1988, RG238 M891/15/0015–33. The value established in the report of the Klein Commission was nearly two million marks lower, a difference accounted for presumably by the addition of further properties or an adjustment in valuation for which there is no evidence: Official Transcript, Trial Evidence Presentation, 23 May 1947, RG238 M891/4/0110. There existed confusion at Flick's trial as to whether the document in question was the actual contract or, in view of subsequent discussions, merely an additional binding draft; for the purposes here, it shall be considered as the final contract.

68. Betr.: Besprechung bei dem Hermann Göring-Werken wegen Lothringer Werke, 19 January 1943, NI-1989, RG238 M891/15/0037–39.

69. Notiz für Herrn Flick, 20 January 1943, NI-2513, RG238 M891/15/0043–46.

70. Notiz für Herrn Flick, 20 January 1943, NI-2513, RG238 M891/15/0043–46.

71. Notiz für Herrn Dr. Flick, Betr.: Rombach/Betriebsüberlassungsvertrag/Steuerfragen, 18 August 1943, RG242 T83/55/3423742–43.

72. On the retroactive date of ownership and other details of the final contract, see the Reichsminister der Finanzen an die Bezirksgruppe der Wirtschaftsgruppe Eisenschaffende Industrie, Betr.: Betriebsüberlassungverträge für die lothringischen Eisen- und Stahlwerke, 8 August 1944, RG242 T83/55/3423696–97.

73. The terms in summary form: Notiz, 2 September 1943, RG242 T83/55/3423741; see the agreement signed on 15 December 1942 by the official responsible for the sequestration of steelworks and by Flick on 17 April 1944: RG242 T83/55/3423716–17.

74. See the arbitration contract signed on 15 December 1942 by the official responsible for sequestration of steelworks and on 17 April 1944 by the Flick concern along: Schiedsvertrag, RG242 T83/55/3423719–20.

75. Betrifft: Betriebsüberlassungvertrag, 1 March 1944, NI-1886, RG238 M891/15/0049–53. According to trial transcript, a conference concerning the contract took place on 17 March 1943, although evidence of the meeting is indirect. The contract most probably took effect on 1 April 1943 based on the indirect evidence of overdue dates for interest payments on the value of the assets: 23 May-M-DJG-5-2-Ninabuck (Lund), RG238 M891/4/0125.

76. Betr.: Reichswerke Hermann Göring, Anteil an der Eisenschaffenden Industrie, 29 May 1941, NI-322, RG238 M891/15/0056–59. The report figured the total output of the industry at 30.6 million tons.

77. Notiz Betr.: Rohstahlerzeugung ohne Salzgitter und Linz, 4 November 1940, NI-4597, RG238 M891/15/0062–63. The trial transcript points out that Flick by this point had surpassed the Krupp concern, a shift as reflective of Krupp's decrease in production as Flick's substantial increase.

Chapter 5. The Significance of Lorraine for the German Steel Industry and the Flick Concern's Administration of the Rombach Works, 1941–1944

1. In addition to officials associated with the Reichswerke, even private businessmen such as Hermann Röchling, considered the leading industrialist of the Saar, argued to Göring as early as 1935 that Germany could not depend on wartime imports of Swedish ore: Riedel, *Eisen und Kohle für das Dritte Reich*, 128–29.

2. Georg Thomas, *Geschichte der deutschen Wehr- und Rüstungswirtschaft (1918–1943/45)*, ed. Wolfgang Birkenfeld (Boppard: Boldt, 1966), 181; Mollin, *Montankonzerne und "Drittes Reich,"* 157ff, 164ff; Jahresbericht des Generalbeauftragten für die Eisenerzgewinnung und –verteilung für die Gebiete Luxemburg und Lothringen für das Jahr 1941, BA R13I/1133.

3. Jahresbericht des Generalbeauftragten für die Eisenerzgewinnung und -verteilung für die Gebiete Luxemburg und Lothringen für das Jahr 1941, BA R13I/1133.

4. Fritz, *German Steel and Swedish Iron Ore*, 15.

5. Müller, "Mobilization of the German Economy," 506–12.

6. Klein notes that scarcely a meeting involving Hitler and his economic advisers occurred between 1939 and 1943 that did not deal in some manner with the steel shortage, which appeared to dwarf all other economic problems: *Germany's Economic Preparations for War*, 114ff.

7. Wirtschaftsgruppe Eisenschaffende Industrie, Eisen und Stahlfragen—Besprechung mit Herrn General von Hanneken, BA R13I/692, 105.

8. Testimony of Flick, 10 July 1947, RG238 M891/5/0404.

9. Aktenvermerk über die Besprechung im Hauptquartier des Generalfeldmarschall Göring v.19.6.1940, PS-1155, RG238 M891/14/1025.

10. Notiz Burkart—Betr.: Besprechung mit Herrn von Hanneken am 10. Juni, 11.6.1940, NI-3516, RG238 M891/14/1155–58; Fritz, *German Steel and Swedish Iron Ore*, 71–76.

11. Alfred C. Mierzejewski, *The Collapse of the German War Economy, 1944–1945: Allied Air Power and the German National Railway* (Chapel Hill: University of North Carolina Press, 1988); Horst Rohde, "Das deutsche Eisenbahnverkehrswesen in der deutschen Kriegswirtschaft 1939-1945," in *Kriegswirtschaft und Rüstung 1939-1945*, ed. Friedrich Forstmeier and Hans-Erich Volkmann (Düsseldorf: Droste Verlag, 1977), 134–63; Klaus Hildebrand, "Die Deutsche Reichsbahn in der Zeit der nationalsozialistischen Diktatur 1933-1945," in *Die Eisenbahn in Deutschland: von den Anfängen bis zur Gegenwart*, ed. Lothar Gall and Manfred Pohl (München: C. H. Beck, 1999), 165–250.

12. As Hanneken of the Economics Ministry aptly put it, "An armed force that cannot move as a result of a deficient rail system . . . is nothing other than an empty balloon." Wirtschaftsgruppe Eisenschaffende Industrie, Eisen und Stahlfragen—Besprechung mit Herrn General von Hanneken, BA R13I/692, 105.

13. Fritz, *German Steel and Swedish Iron Ore*, 86–87, especially note 30.

14. See the alleged decision to purchase at inflated prices two sintering works for the processing of raw ore for the HGW's Hayingen operation at a time when most works questioned their economic utility entirely: Letter of O.-E. Flick to Burkart, Betrifft: Investitionsplan für die Kalenderjahre 1944 and 1945, 11 May 1944, RG242 T83/55/3423653–58.

15. The problem of the Reichswerke's redundant capacity is discussed in Notiz Betr.: Besprechung mit Herrn von Hanneken am 10. Juni, 11 June 1940, NI-3516, RG238 M891/14/0155–58.

16. Aktennotiz der Wehrwirtschaftsstab des OKW über eine Besprechung am 1. November 1939 über die Planung der Eisen- und Stahlproduktion, in Eichholtz and Schumann, *Anatomie des Krieges*, 228.

17. Ibid., 229.

18. An excellent survey of Flick's trusteeship is Johanes Bähr, "Die Rombacher Hüttenwerke unter der Treuhänderschaft Flicks," in Bähr et al., *Flick Konzern*, 451–62.

19. Testimony of Burkart, 4 September 1947, RG238 M891/25/0748.

20. Bericht—vorgenommene Prüfung der wirtschaftlichen und steuerlchen Verhältnisse bei der Rombacher Hüttenwerke, 29 August 1941, RG242 T83/55/3423888–910.

21. Deposition of Jean-Pierre Kieffer, 16 July 1947, Bu-193, RG238 M891/31/0177.

22. Testimony of Röchling, 15 September 1947, RG238 M891/26/0377.

23. Testimony of Burkart, 4 September 1947, RG238 M891/25/0749.

24. Ibid.

25. Affidavit of Paul Raabe, 27 May 1947, Bu-829, RG238 M891/31/0185.

26. The integrity of the process whereby the Klein Commission arrived at its estimate of the plant's total value cannot be ascertained from the available evidence.

27. Testimony of Flick, 10 July 1947, RG238 M891/23/0056–57; Flick's brazenly uncomprehending tone in his postwar testimony, which suggested that he was more to be commended for his magnanimity than condemned for his rapaciousness, is striking.

28. Aktennotiz für Herrn Direktor Dr. Hanemann, Betr.: Investition, 26 November 1943, RG242 T83/55/3423411–12. Walter Hanemann was a *Prokurist*, or official with full power of attorney, for the Rombacher Hüttenwerke: Beglaubigte Abschrift aus dem Handelsregister, RG242 T83/55/3423867.

29. Anordnung zur Sicherstellung des planmässigen Ausbaues der Eisenindustrie in Lothringen, 14 November 1941, Nr. 630, *Verordnungsblatt für Lothringen*, 1941, 1006.

30. Notiz Betr.: Reichsamt für Wirtschaftsausbau—Neubauanträge, 27 February 1942, RG242 T83/55/3423335–39. The munitions office handled cases involving steel for infrastructural construction purposes, a very large category, and presumably also for highly specialized forms of munitions-grade metal.

31. Der Reichs- und Preußische Wirtschaftsminister, Richtlinien für die Stellung von Anträgen, 5 November 1937, RG242 T83/55/3423340.

32. Letter of Flick to Burkart, 8 March 1942, Betr.: Neubauten, RG242 T83/55/3423298–99; see the appended listing labeled "Vordringliche Neubauten."

33. See the detailed report and cost summary submitted by O.-E. Flick to his father as chairman of the supervisory board on 15 August 1942: Finanzplan für Neubauten in Rombach, RG242 T83/55/3423445–47.

34. Letter of Flick to Burkart, 7 April 1942, Betr.: Erweiterung und Erneuerung der Werksanlagen—Genehmigung durch den CdZ–Unser Schrieben vom 19.1.1942, RG242 T83/55/3423296; on the Reichswerke's distortion of priorities, see Overy, *Goering*, 98.

35. See the appended comments to the letter of Burkart to Otto-Ernst Flick, 5 March 1942, Betr.: Neubaufragen für Rombach, RG242 T83/55/3423300–7.

36. Letter of O.-E. Flick to Burkart, Betr.: Investierung Rombach, 27 August 1943, RG242 T83/55/3423422–23; Letter of O.-E. Flick to Wenner, Betr.: Erweiterung und Erneuerung von Werksanlagen, 17 August 1943, RG242 T83/55/3423419–20; and Wenner's approval on behalf of the civil administrator on 20 September 1943, RG242 T83/55/3423416. The sintering equipment, considered a poor investment by O.-E. Flick, generated substantial cost overruns that led to his father's later hesitation to approve any new investment programs for Rombach: Letter of O.-E. Flick to Burkart, Betr.: Investitionsplan für die Kalenderjahre 1944 und 1945, 11 May 1944, RG242 T83/55/3423653–58.

37. Letter of O.-E. Flick to Wenner, Betr.: Erweiterung und Erneuerung von Werksanlagen.—Errichtung eines 80t SM-Ofens, 28 October 1943, RG242 T83/55/3423410; and Wenner's approval on behalf of the civil administrator on 18 January 1944, RG242 T83/55/3423407.

38. Letter of O.-E. Flick to Burkart, Betr.: Investitionsplan für die Kalenderjahre 1944 and 1945, 11 May 1944, RG242 T83/55/3423653; Notiz für Herrn Direktor Geschwinde, 22 June 1944, RG242 T83/55/3423651. Herbert Geschwinde was a *Prokurist*, or official with full power of attorney, for the Rombacher Hüttenwerke: Beglaubigte Abschrift aus dem Handelsregister, RG242 T83/55/3423867.

39. The best summary is a detailed letter and group of tables from the Rombacher Hüttenwerke to Wenner: Neuinvestierungen in Rombach, 29 June 1944, RG242 T83/55/3423677–83.

40. Selbstkosten- und Ergebnislage Rombach, 10 April 1943, NI-6000, RG238 M891/13/0329–40. Portions of this critical microfilmed document are regrettably unreadable.

41. Ibid.

42. The standard work on forced labor in the economy of Nazi Germany is Ulrich Herbert, *Hitler's Foreign Workers: Enforced Foreign Labor in Germany under the Third Reich* (Cambridge: Cambridge University Press, 1997).

43. Mark Spoerer and Jochen Fleischhacker, "Forced Laborers in Nazi Germany: Categories, Numbers, and Survivors," *Journal of Interdisciplinary History* 33 (2002), 176, offers a useful typology based on distinctions between conditions of life and work.

44. Verordnung über die Sicherung des Gefolgschaftsstandes in der Kriegswirtschaft, 20 May 1942, RG238 M891/34/0929.

45. Deposition of Karl Raabe, 14 November 1946, Fl-93, RG238 M891/31/0533–34; Herbert, *Foreign Workers*, 130–31, 293.

46. Letter of O.-E. Flick to Burkart, Betrifft: Investierung Rombach, 27 August 1943, RG242 T83/55/3423422–23.

47. Marcel Neigert, *Internements et déportation en Moselle, 1940–1945* (Metz: Centre de Recherches Relations Internationals de l'Université de Metz, 1978), 23.

48. Friedrich Franz to Flick, 4 November 1944, NI-5592, RG238 M891/13/0345; the labor force by that point consisted of 2,800 "Reichs- und Volksdeutschen, meist Lothringen," 1,400 foreigners (chiefly Italians, Russians, and Poles), 200 Russian prisoners of war, and 1,800 male and female "Ostarbeiter." The greater portion of the report is regrettably unreadable.

49. Bericht—vorgenommene Prüfung der wirtschaftlichen und steuerlchen Verhältnisse bei der Rombacher Hüttenwerke, 29 August 1941, RG242 T83/55/3423888–910.

50. Richtlinien für die kommissarischen Verwalter der Eisenhütten von Lothringen und Meurthe-et-Moselle vom 5 Juli 1940, BU-819, RG238 M891/31/0096–99.

51. Bericht über Rombacher Hüttenwerke G.m.b.H. von Direktor Franz, NI-1656/5592, RG238 M891/13/0343–46.

52. Selbstkosten- und Ergebnislage Rombach, 10 April 1943, NI-6000, RG238 M891/13/0329.

53. Ibid.

54. Selbstkosten- und Ergebnislage Rombach, 10 April 1943, NI-6000, RG238 M891/13/0331.

55. Letter of O.-E. Flick to Burkart, Betr.: Investitionsplan für die Kalenderjahre 1944 and 1945, 11 May 1944, RG242 T83/55/3423657–58; on the transportation impasse, also Burkart's reply, 21 June 1944, RG242 T83/55/3423685. The coke supply had apparently always been inadequate to the demand; a 1941 financial audit revealed only five of eight furnaces in operation: Bericht—vorgenommene Prüfung der wirtschaftlichen und steuerlichen Verhältnisse bei der Rombacher Hüttenwerke, 29 August 1941, RG242 T83/55/3423888–910.

56. Affidavit of Paul Raabe, 27 May 1947, Bu-829, RG238 M891/31/0185.

57. Testimony of Flick, RG238 M891/23/0062.

58. Betr.: Wehrwirtschaftliche Fertigung, 3 February 1943, NI-3949, RG238 M891/15/0070–72.

59. Betr.: Champagne sur Seine, 20 August 1943, NI-4998, RG238 M891/15/0085–87.

60. Betr.: Ernennung von Patenfirmen in Frankreich, 2 December 1943, NI-5461, RG238 M891/15/0090–107, contains a comprehensive list of the sponsored French firms. This document was acquired surreptitiously by O.-E. Flick from the chief of staff to the German armaments representative in Paris.

61. Testimony of Burkart, 4 September 1947, RG238 M891/25/0751–52.

62. Errichtung eines SM.-Ofens in Rombach, 4 February 1943, NI-3949, RG238 M891/15/0067.

63. Betr.: Wehrwirtschaftliche Fertigung, 3 February 1943, NI-3949, RG238 M891/15/0070–72.

64. Betr.: Champagne sur Seine, 20 August 1943, NI-4998, RG238 M891/15/0085–87.

65. Unfortunately, the available evidence is insufficient to ascertain consistently the level of steel output at Rombach in absolute or comparative terms, and so does not support conclusions regarding the significance of Flick's acquisition in that respect for his concern or the war economy as a whole.

66. Notiz für Kaletsch, Betr.: Rombach, 15 September 1944, RG242 T83/55/3423930–31; the *Anlage* consists of a detailed account of the funds transferred.

67. Testimony of Flick, 10 July 1947, *TWC*, 940.

Conclusion

1. See the discussion in Overy, *Goering*, 123–25.

2. James, *The Deutsche Bank and the Nazi Economic War Against the Jews*, 213.

3. Ibid., 214.

4. Testimony of Flick, 10 July 1947, *TWC*, 947.

5. Hayes, *Industry and Ideology*, 319.

6. Richard Tilly, review of Milward, *Journal of Economic History* 34 (1974), 513; Milward, *The French Economy*, 100.

BIBLIOGRAPHY

Primary Sources

Bundesarchiv, Berlin (BA)

R3—*Reichsministerium für Rüstung und Kriegsproduktion*

R13I—*Wirtschaftsgruppe Eisenschaffende Industrie*

R1501—*Reichsministerium des Innern*

Bundesarchiv-Militärarchiv, Freiburg (BA-MA)

   RW4—*Wehrmachtführungsstab*

   RW19—*Wirtschafts- und Rüstungsamtes (WiRüAmt)*

   RW31—*OKW/WiRüAmt/Wirtschaftsstab Ost*

   RW35—*Militärbefehlshaber Frankreich*

Chef der Zivilverwanltung in Lothringen, *Verordnungsblatt für Lothringen (VbfL)*. Saarbrücken, 1940.

Documents on German Foreign Policy, 1918–1945. Series D, vol. 7. Washington, DC: U.S. Government Printing Office, 1959–83.

Miscellaneous German Records Collection, 1892–1945. United States National Archives—Collection of Seized Enemy Records. Record Group (RG) 242, Series T84.

Records of Private German Enterprises and Individuals. United States National Archives—Collection of Seized Enemy Records. Record Group (RG) 242, Series T83.

Records of the Reich Ministry of Economics. United States National Archives—Collection of Seized Enemy Records. Record Group (RG) 242, Series T71.

Trials of War Criminals before the Nuernberg Military Tribunals under Control Council Law No. 10 (TWC), vol. VI. Washington, DC: U.S. Government Printing Office, 1952.

United States of America v *Friedrich Flick et al.* (Case 5) 8 February 1947– 22 December 1947. United States National Archives—World War Two War Crimes Records. Record Group (RG) 238, Series M891.

Secondary Sources

Aalders, Gerald. "Three Ways of German Economic Penetration in the Netherlands: Cloaking, Capital Interlocking, and 'Aryanization.'" In *Die "Neuordnung Europas": NS-Wirtschaftspolitik in den besetzten Gebieten*, ed. Richard J. Overy. Berlin: Metropol, 1997.

Anneser, Jules. *Vautours sur la Lorraine: Documents inédits sur l'occupation en Lorraine rassemblés et commentés*. Metz: Éditions le Lorrain, 1948.

Bajak, Curtis. "The Third Reich's Corporation Law of 1937." Dissertation, Yale University, 1986.

Bajohr, Frank. *"Aryanization" in Hamburg: The Economic Exclusion of Jews and the Confiscation of Their Property in Nazi Germany*. New York: Berghahn, 2002.

———. "The 'Aryanization' of Jewish Companies and German Society: The Example of Hamburg." In *International Conference: German Society's Response to Nazi Anti-Jewish Policy 1933–1941*. Yad Vashem, 10–13 February 1995.

———. "The Beneficiaries of 'Aryanization': Hamburg as a Case Study." In *Yad Vashem Studies* 26, 1998.

Barkai, Avraham. "German Entrepreneurs and Jewish Policy in the Third Reich." In *Yad Vashem Studies* 21, 1991.

———. *Nazi Economics: Ideology, Theory, and Policy*. New Haven: Yale University Press, 1990.

———. "Sozialdarwinismus und Antiliberalismus in Hitlers Wirtschafts-konzept: Zu Henry A. Turner Jr., Hitlers Einstellung zu Wirtschaft und Gesellschaft vor 1933." In *Geschichte und Gesellschaft* 3, 1977.

Berthold, Rudolf. *Produktivekräfte in Deutschland 1917/8 bis 1945*. Berlin: Akademie Verlag, 1988.

Beyschlag, F., and P. Krusch, *Deutschlands künftige Versorgung mit Eisen- und Mangenerzen*. Berlin, 1917.

Böhme, Hermann. *Der deutsche-französische Waffenstillstand im Zweiten Weltkrieg*. Stuttgart: Deutsche Verlagsanstalt, 1966.

Bohn, Robert. *Reichskommissariat Norwegen: "Nationalsozialistische Neu-ordnung" und Kriegswirtschaft*. München: Oldenbourg Wissenschafts-verlag, 2000.

Bracher, Karl-Dietrich. *Die deutsche Diktatur: Enstehung, Struktur, Folgen des Nationalsozialismus.* Köln: Kiepenheuer und Witsch, 1970.

Buchmann, Erich. *Von der jüdischen Firma Simson zur Nationalsozilialistischer Industriestiftung Gustloff Werke,* Thüringer Untersuchungen zur Judenfrage 10. Erfurt: U. Bodung, 1944.

Carroll, B. A. *Design for Total War: Arms and Economics in the Third Reich.* The Hague: Mouton, 1968.

Domarus, Max. *Hitler: Speeches and Proclamations 1932–1945: The Chronicle of a Dictatorship,* vol. 2, *1935–1938.* Wauconda, IL: Bolchazy-Carducci, 1992.

Döring, Diether. *Die deutschen Schwerindustriellen Interessen in Lothringen bis 1914.* Frankfurt am Main, 1971.

Drobisch, Klaus. "Dokumente zur direkten Zusammenarbeit zwischen Flick-Konzern und Gestapo bein der Unterdrückung der Arbeiter." In *Jahrbuch für Wirtschaftsgeschichte* 3, 1963.

———. "Flick und die Nazis." In *Zeitschrift für Geschichtswissenschaft* 14, 1966.

———. "Flick-Konzern und faschistischen Staat, 1933–1939." In *Monopole und Staat in Deutschland, 1917–1945.* Edited by Karl Drechsler. Berlin: Akademie Verlag, 1966.

Eichholtz, Dietrich. "Das Minette-Revier und die deutsche Montanindustrie. Zur Strategie der deutschen Monopole im zweiten Weltkrieg 1941/42." In *Zeitschrift für Geschichtswissenschaft* 25, 1977.

———. *Geschichte der deutschen Kriegswirtschaft 1939–1945,* vol. 1, *1939–1941.* Berlin: Akademie Verlag, 1984.

Erker, Paul. "Aufbruch zu neuen Paradigmen: Unternehmensgeschichte zwischen sozialgeschichtlicher und betriebswirtschaftlicher Erweiterung." In *Archiv für Sozialgeschichte* 37, 1997.

Ernst, Robert. *Rechenschaftsbericht eines Elsässers.* Berlin: Bernard und Graefe, 1954.

Fall 5. Anklageplädoyer, ausgewählte Dokumente Urteil des Flick-Prozesses. Edited by Karl-Heinz Thieleke. Berlin: Deutsche Verlag der Wissenschaften, 1965.

Feldenkirchen, Wilfried. *Die Eisen- und Stahlindustrie des Ruhrgebiets 1879–1914. Wachstum, Finanzierung und Unternehmensstruktur ihrer*

Großunternehmen, Beiheft 20, *Zeitschrift für Unternehmensgeschichte*. Wiesbaden: Steiner, 1982.

Feldman, Gerald. *Iron and Steel in the German inflation, 1916–1923*. Princeton: Princeton University Press, 1977.

Fischer, Wolfram. *Deutsche Wirtschaftspolitik 1918-1945*, 3rd ed. Opladen: C. W. Leske, 1968.

Fonderies de fonte et d'acier. Edited by Société d'éditions géographiques professionelles. Paris, 1971.

Francois-Poncet, Andre. *The Fateful Years. Memoirs of a French Ambassaor in Berlin, 1931–1938*. New York: Harcourt, Brace, 1949.

Fritz, Martin. *German Steel and Swedish Iron Ore, 1939–1945*. Göteborg: Institute of Economic History of Gothenburg University, 1974.

Genschel, Helmut. *Die Verdrängung der Juden aus der Wirtschaft im Dritten Reich*. Göttingen: Musterschmidt Verlag, 1966.

German Designs on French Lorraine: The Secret Memorandum of the German Iron and Steel Manufacturers. London: G. Allen & Unwin, 1918.

Giltner, Philip. *"In the Friendliest Manner": German-Danish Economic Cooperation during the Nazi Occupation 1940–1945*. New York: P. Lang, 1998.

Gruchmann, Lothar. *Nationalsozialistische Grossraumordnung: Die Konstruktion einer "deutschen Monroe-Doktrin."* Stuttgart: Deutsche Verlags-Anstalt, 1962.

Haus, Rainer. *Lothringen und Salzgitter in der Eisenerzpolitik der deutschen Schwerindustrie von 1971–1940*. Edited by Archiv der Stadt Salzgitter. *Salzgitter Forschungen*, vol. 1. Salzgitter: Archiv der Stadt Salzgitter, 1991.

Hayes, Peter. "Big Business and 'Aryanization' in Germany, 1933–1939." In *Jahrbuch für Antisemitismusforschung* 3, 1994.

———. "Carl Bosch and Carl Krauch: Chemistry and the Political Economy of Germany 1925–1945." In *Journal of Economic History* 47, 1987.

———. *From Cooperation to Complicity: Degussa in the Third Reich*. Cambridge: Cambridge University Press, 2004.

———. "Industrie und Ideologie: Die IG Farben in der Zeit des Nationalsozialismus." In *Zeitschrift für Unternehmensgeschichte* 32, 1987.

———. *Industry and Ideology: IG Farben in the Nazi Era*. Cambridge: Cambridge University Press, 1987.

———. "Polycracy and Policy in the Third Reich: The Case of the Economy." In *Reevaluating the Third Reich*. Edited by Thomas Childers and Jane Caplan. New York: Holmes & Meier, 1993.

Herbert, Ulrich. *Hitler's Foreign Workers: Enforced Foreign Labor in Germany under the Third Reich*. Cambridge: Cambridge University Press, 1997.

Hildebrand, Klaus. *The Foreign Policy of the Third Reich*. Berkeley: University of California Press, 1973.

Hillgruber, Andreas. "Frankreich als Faktor der deutschen Außenpolitik im Jahre 1939." Franco-German historical symposium in Bonn, 26–29 September 1978.

———. *Hitlers Strategie: Politik und Kriegführung, 1940–1941*. Frankfurt am Main: Bernard & Graefe Verlag für Wehrwesen, 1965.

Hitler, Adolf. *Hitlers Zweites Buch. Ein Dokument aus dem Jahr 1928*. Introduction and commentary by Gerhard Weinberg. Stuttgart: Deutsche Verlags-Anstalt, 1961.

———. *Mein Kampf*. Translated by Ralph Manheim. Boston: Houghton Mifflin, 1943.

———. *Monologe im Führer-Hauptquartier, 1941–1944*. Edited by Werner Jochmann. Hamburg: A. Knaus, 1980.

Hofer, Walter. *Die Entfesselung des Zweiten Weltkrieges. Eine Studie über die internationalen Beziehungen im Sommer 1939 mit Dokumenten*. Frankfurt am Main: Fischer Bücherei, 1963.

Hörster-Philipps, Ulrike. *Im Schatten des grossen Geldes. Flick-Konzern und Politik: Weimarer Republik, Drittes Reich, Bundesrepublik*. Köln: Pahl Rugenstein, 1985.

Houwink ten Cate, Johannes. "Die rüstungswirtschaftliche Ausnutzung Westeuropas während der ersten Kriegshälfte." In *Das organisierte Chaos. "Ämterdarwinismus" und "Gesinnungsethik." Determinanten nationalsozialistischer Besatzungsherrschaft*. Edited by Gerhard Otto and Johannes Th. M. Houwink ten Cate. Berlin: Metropol, 1999.

Hüttenberger, Peter. "Nationalsozialistische Polykratie." In *Geschichte und Gesellschaft* 2, 1976.

Jäckel, Eberhard. *Frankreich in Hitlers Europa: Die deutsche Frankreichpolitik im Zweiten Weltkrieg.* Stuttgart: Deutsche Verlags-Anstalt, 1966.

———. *Hitlers World View: A Blueprint for Power.* Cambridge: Harvard University Press, 1981.

Jacobsen, Hans-Adolf. *Nationalsozialistische Außenpolitik 1933–1938.* Frankfurt am Main: A. Metzner, 1968.

Jäger, Jorg-Johannes. *Die wirtschaftliche Abhängigkeit des Dritten Reichs vom Ausland dargestellt am Beispiel der Stahlindustrie.* Berlin: Berlin Verlag, 1969.

James, Harold. "Die Deutsche Bank und die Diktatur 1933-1945." In *Die Deutsche Bank 1870–1945.* Edited by Lothar Gall et al. München: Beck, 1995.

———. *The Deutsche Bank and the Nazi Economic War against the Jews: The Expropriation of Jewish-owned Property.* Cambridge: Cambridge University Press, 2001.

Jochmann, Werner, ed. *Monologe im Führer-Hauptquartier, 1941–1944.* Hamburg: A. Knaus, 1980.

Kettenacker, Lothar. *Nationalsozialistische Volkstumspolitik im Elsaß.* Stuttgart: Deutsche Verlags-Anstalt, 1973.

Klein, Burton H. *Germany's Economic Preparations for War.* Cambridge: Harvard University Press, 1959.

Kluke, Paul. "Nationalsozialistische Europaideologie." In *Vierteljahrshefte für Zeitgeschichte* 3, 1955.

———. "Nationalsozialistische Volkstumspolitik in Elsaß-Lothringen 1940–1945." In *Zur Geschichte und Problematik der Demokratie. Festgabe für Hans Herzfeld.* Edited by Carl Hinrichs and Wilhelm Berges. Berlin: Duncker und Humblot, 1958.

Knipping, Franz. "Frankreich in Hitlers Außenpolitik 1933-1939." In *Hitler, Deutschland und die Mächte: Materialien zur Außenpolitik des Dritten Reiches.* Edited by Manfred Funke. Düsseldorf: Droste Verlag, 1976.

Köhler, Henning. "Zum Verhältnis Friedrich Flicks zur Reichsregierung am Ende der Weimarer Republik." In *Industrielles System und politische Entwicklung in der Weimarer Republik.* Edited by Hans

Mommsen, Dietmar Petzina, and Bernd Weisbrod. Düsseldorf: Droste Verlag, 1974.

Kratzsch, Gerhard. *Der Gauwirtschaftsapparat der NSDAP: Menschenführung—"Arisierung"—Wehrwirtschaft im Gau Westfalen-Süd. Eine Studie zur Herrschaftspraxis im totalitären Staat.* Münster: Aschendorff, 1989.

Kuhn, Axel. *Hitlers außenpolitisches Programm: Entstehung und Entwicklung 1919–1933.* Stuttgart: Klett, 1970.

Lochner, Louis. *Tycoons and Tyrant: German Industry from Hitler to Adenauer.* Chicago: H. Regnery, 1954.

Mason, Tim. *Social Policy in the Third Reich: The Working Class and the "National Community."* Providence, Oxford: Berg, 1993.

May, Ernest. *Strange Victory: Hitler's Conquest of France.* New York: Hill & Wang, 2000.

Messerschmidt, Manfred. "Foreign Policy and Preparation for War." In Wilhelm Deist, Manfred Messerschmidt, Hans-Erich Volkmann, and Wolfram Wette. *Germany and the Second World War*, vol. 1, *The Build-up of German Aggression.* Oxford: Oxford University Press, 1990.

Mierzejewski, Alfred S. *The Collapse of the German War Economy, 1944–1945: Allied Air Power and the German National Railway.* Chapel Hill: University of North Carolina Press, 1988.

Milward, Alan S. "Bericht." In *Industrielles System und politische Entwicklung in der Weimarer Republik*, vol. 1. Edited by H. Mommsen, D. Petzina, and B. Weisbrod. Düsseldorf: Droste Verlag, 1974.

———. "Could Sweden Have Stopped the Second World War?" In *The Scandanavian Economic Review* 15, 1967.

———. *The New Order and the French Economy.* Oxford: Oxford University Press, 1970.

Mollin, Gerhard Thomas. "Der Strukturwandel der Montanindustrie in der NS-Wirtschaft." In *Der Zweite Weltkrieg: Analysen, Grundzüge, Forschungsbilanz.* Edited by Wolfgang Michalka. Munich: Piper, 1989.

———. *Montankonzerne und "Drittes Reich": Der Gegensatz zwischen Monopolindustrie und Befehlswirtschaft in der deutschen Rüstung und Expansion 1936-1944.* Göttingen: Vandenhoeck & Ruprecht, 1988.

Mönnich, Horst. *Labyrinthe der Macht. 3 Geschichten vom Kapital: Stinnes, Thyssen, Flick.* Frankfurt am Main: Umschau Verlag, 1975.

Müller, Rolf-Dieter. "The Failure of the Economic 'Blitzkrieg Strategy." In *Germany and the Second World War*, vol. IV, *The Attack on the Soviet Union.* Edited by Horst Boog, Jürgen Förster, Jürgen Hoffmann, Ernst Klink, Rolf-Dieter Müller, and Gerhard Ueberschär. Oxford: Oxford University Press, 1998.

Müller, Rolf-Dieter, Bernhard Kroener, and Hans Umbreit. "The Mobilization of the German Economy for Hitler's War Aims." In *Germany and the Second World War*, vol. V/I, *Organization and Mobilization of the German Sphere of Power.* Oxford: Oxford University Press, 2000.

Müller-Hillebrand, Burkhart. *Das Heer 1933–1945. Entwicklung des organisatorischen Aufbaus,* vol. 1, *Das Heer bis zum Kriegsbeginn.* Darmstadt: E. S. Mittler, 1956.

Murray, Williamson. *The Change in the European Balance of Power, 1938–1939: The Path to Ruin.* Princeton: Princeton University Press, 1984.

Nazi Conspiracy and Aggression, vol. 7 (Washington, DC: U.S. Government Printing Office, 1946.

Neebe, Reinhard. "Die Industrie und der 30. Januar 1933." In *Nationalsozialistische Diktatur 1933–1945. Eine Bilanz.* Edited by K.-D. Bracher, Manfred Funke, and H.-A. Jacobsen. Bonn: Bundeszentrale für politische Bildung, 1983.

Neigert, Marcel. *Internements et déportation en Moselle, 1940–1945.* Metz: Centre de Recherches Relations Internationals de l'Université de Metz, 1978.

Nievelstein, Markus. *Der Zug nach der Minette: Deutsche Unternehmen in Lothringen, 1871–1918. Handlungsspielräume und Strategien im Spannungsfeld des deutsch-französisichen Grenzgebietes.* Bochum: N. Brockmeyer, 1993.

Noakes, Jeremy. "'Viceroys of the Reich?' *Gauleiters* 1925–45." In *Working towards the Führer.* Edited by Anthony McElligott and Tim Kirk. Manchester: Manchester University Press, 2003.

Ogger, Günter. *Friedrich Flick der Große.* Bern: Droemer Knaur, 1971.

Overy, Richard J. *Goering: "The Iron Man."* London: Routledge and Kegan Paul, 1984.

———. *The Nazi Economic Recovery 1932–1938*, 2nd ed. Cambridge: Cambridge University Press, 1996.

———. *War and Economy in the Third Reich.* Oxford: Oxford University Press, 1994.

Petzina, Dieter. *Autarkiepolitik im Dritten Reich: Der nationalsozialistische Vierjahresplan.* Stuttgart: Deutsche Verlags-Anstalt, 1968.

Phelps, Reginald. "Hitler als Parteiredner im Jahre 1920." In *Vierteljahrshefte für Zeitgeschichte* 2, 1963.

Pinner, Felix. *Deutsche Wirtschaftsführer.* Charlottenburg: Weltbühne, 1924.

Propaganda and Aryanization, 1938–1944. New York: Garland, 1982.

Raabe, Paul. "Das Lothringische Minette-Gebiet und seine wirtschaftliche Bedeutung." In *Stahl und Eisen* 61/2, 9 January 1941.

Ramge, Thomas. *Die Flicks: Eine deutsche Familiengeschichte um Geld, Macht und Politik.* Frankfurt am Main: Campus Verlag, 2004.

Rauecker, Bruno. *Die sozialen und wirtschaftlichen Beziehungen zwischen Elsass-Lothringen und dem Saargebiet, 1920–1945.* Heidelberg: K. Vowinckel, 1937.

Rauschning, Hermann. *Gespräche mit Hitler.* Wien: Europaverlag, 1973.

Rebentisch, Dieter and Karl Teppe. *Verwaltung contra Menschenführung im Staat Hitlers. Studien zum politisch-administrativen System.* Göttingen: Vandenhoeck und Ruprecht, 1986.

Reckendrees, Alfred. *Das "Stahltrust"-Projekt: Die Gründung der Vereinigte Stahlwerke AG und ihre Unternehmensentwicklung 1926–1933/34.* München: C. H. Beck, 2000.

Recker, Marie-Luise. *Die Aussenpolitik des Dritten Reiches.* München: R. Oldenbourg, 1990.

Rheinländer, Paul. *Die deutsche Eisen- und Stahlwirtschaft im Vierjahresplan.* Berlin: Junker und Dünnhaupt, 1939.

Rich, Norman. *Hitler's War Aims: Ideology, the Nazi State, and the Course of Expansion.* New York: W. W. Norton & Company, 1973.

Riedel, Matthias. *Eisen und Kohle für das Dritte Reich: Paul Pleigers Stellung in der NS-Wirtschaft.* Göttingen: Musterschmidt, 1973.

Röchling, Hermann. "Lothringens Eisenindustrie." In *Stahl und Eisen* 61/2, 9 January 1941.

——. *Wir Halten die Saar!* Berlin: Volk und Reich Verlag, 1934.

Rohde, Horst. "Das deutsche Eisenbahnverkehrswesen in der deutschen Kriegswirtschaft 1939–1945." In *Kriegswirtschaft und Rüstung 1939–1945*. Edited by Friedrich Forstmeier and Hans-Erich Volkmann. Düsseldorf: Droste, 1977.

Rousseau, Armelle. *De fonte et d'acier*. Thionville: G. Klopp, 1995.

Salewski, Michael. "National Socialist Ideas on Europe." In *Documents on the History of European Integration*. Edited by Walter Lipgens, vol. 1, *Continental Plans for European Union 1939–1945*. Berlin: Walter de Gruyter, 1985.

Schärer, Martin R. *Deutsche Annexionspolitik im Westen. Die Wiedereingliederung Eupen-Malmedys im zweiten Weltkrieg*, 2nd ed. Bern: Lang, 1978.

Schausberger, Norbert. "Wirtschaftliche Aspekte des Anschlusses Österreichs an das Deutsche Reich: Ein Dokumentation." In *Militärgeschichtliche Mitteilungen* 8, 1970.

Schneider, Michael. "Nationalsozialistische Durchdringung von Staat, Wirtschaft und Gesellschaft. Zur Sozialgeschichte des Dritten Reiches." In *Archiv für Sozialgeschichte* 31, 1991.

Schoenbaum, David. *Hitler's Social Revolution: Class and Status in Nazi Germany 1933–1939*. New York/London: W. W. Norton & Company, 1980.

Schramm, Wilhelm von. *Sprich vom Frieden, wenn du Krieg willst: Die psychologischen Offensiven Hitlers gegen die Franzosen 1933 bis 1939*. Mainz: Hase und Koehler, 1973.

Schubert, Günter. *Anfänge nationalsozialistische Außenpolitik*. Köln: Verlag Wissenschaft und Politik, 1963.

Simpson, Alan. "The Struggle for Control of the German Economy, 1936–37." In *Journal of Modern History* 21, 1959.

Spoerer, Mark. *Von Scheingewinn zum Rüstungsboom: Die Eigenkapitalrentabilität der deutschen Industrieaktiengesellschaften 1925–1941*. Stuttgart: Franz Steiner Verlag, 1996.

Spoerer, Mark, and Jochen Fleischhacker. "Forced Laborers in Nazi Germany: Categories, Numbers, and Survivors." In *Journal of Interdisciplinary History* 33, 2002.

Stallbaumer, Lisa. "Strictly Business? The Flick Concern and "Aryanization": Corporate Expansion in the Nazi Era." Dissertation, University of Wisconsin–Madison, 1995.

Teichert, Eckart. *Autarkie und Großraumwirtschaft in Deutschland 1930–1939: Außenwirtschaftspolitische Kozeptionen zwischen Wirtschaftskrise und Zweitem Weltkrieg.* München: Oldenbourg, 1984.

Thielecke, Karl-Heinz, ed. *Fall 5: Anklageplädoyer, ausgewählte Dokumente, Urteil des Flick-Prozesses.* Berlin: Deutsche Verlag der Wissenschaften, 1965.

Thies, Jochen. *Architekt der Weltherrschaft: Die Endziele Hitlers.* Düsseldorf: Droste, 1976.

Thomas, Georg. *Geschichte der deutschen Wehr- und Rüstungswirtschaft (1918–1943/45).* Edited by Wolfgang Birkenfeld. Boppard: Boldt, 1966.

Tilly, Richard. Review of Alan S. Milward, *The New Order and the French Economy.* In *Journal of Economic History* 34, 1974.

Treue, Wilhelm. "Hitlers Denkschrift zum Vierjahresplan 1936." In *Vierteljahrshefte für Zeitgeschichte* 3, 1955.

———. "Widerstand von Unternehmern und Nationalökonomen." In *Der Widerstand gegen den Nationalsozialismus.* Edited by Jürgen Schmädeke and Peter Steinbach. München: Piper, 1986.

Treue, Wilhelm, and Helmut Uebbing. *Die feuer verlöschen nie: August Thyssen-Hütte 1926–1966.* Düsseldorf: Econ Verlag, 1966.

Trials of War Criminals before the Nuernberg Military Tribunals under Control Council Law No. 10, vol. VI (Washington, DC: U.S. Government Printing Office, 1952.

Turner, Henry Ashby, Jr. *German Big Business and the Rise of Hitler.* Oxford: Oxford University Press, 1985.

———. "Hitlers Einstellung zu Wirtschaft und Gesellschaft vor 1933." In *Geschichte und Gesellschaft* 2, 1976.

———. *Stresemann and the Politics of the Weimar Republic.* Princeton: Princeton University Press, 1963.

Ufermann, Paul. *Der deutsche Stahltrust.* Berlin: Verlagsgesellschaft des Allgemeinen Deutschen Gewerkschaftsbundes, 1927.

Umbreit, Hans. "Nationalsozialistische Expansion 1938–1941: Strukturen der deutschen Besatzungsverwaltungen im Zweiten Weltkrieg."

In Michael Salewski and Josef Schröder, eds., *Dienst für die Geschichte: Gedenkschrift für Walther Hubatsch, 17 Mai 1915–29 Dezember 1984*. Göttingen: Musterschmidt, 1985.

Vogelsang, Reinhard. *Der Freundeskreis Himmler*. Göttingen: Musterschmidt, 1976.

Volkland, Gerhard. "Hintergründe und politische Auswirkungen der Gelsenkirchen-Affäre im Jahre 1932." In *Zeitschrift für Geschichtswissenschaft* 11, 1963.

Volkmann, Hans-Erich. "Aussenhandel und Aufrüstung in Deutschland, 1933 bis 1939." In Friedrich Forstmeier and Hans-Erich Volkmann, eds., *Wirtschaft und Rüstung am Vorabend des Zweiten Weltkrieges*. Düsseldorf: Droste, 1975.

———. "Autarkie, Großraumwirtschaft und Aggression. Zur ökonomischen Motivation der Besetzung Luxemburgs, Belgiens und der Niederlände 1940." In *Militärgeschichtliche Mitteilungen* 14, 1976.

———. "L'importance économique de la Lorraine pour le IIIe Reich." In *Revue d'histoire de la deuxième guerre mondiale* 120, 1980.

Wagenführ, Rolf. *Die deutsche Industrie im Kriege 1939–1945*, 2nd ed. Berlin: Duncker und Humblot, 1963.

Weber, Wolfram. *Die innere Sicherheit im besetzten Belgien und Nordfrankreich 1940–1944: Ein Beitrag zur Geschichte der Besatzungsverwaltungen*. Düsseldorf: Droste, 1978.

Wedding, Hermann. "Die Eisenerzvorräte Deutschlands." In *Verhandlungen des Vereins zur Beförderung des Gewerbfleißes* 86, 1907.

Weinberg, Gerhard. "Secret Hitler-Benes Negotiations in 1936–1937." In *Journal of Central European Affairs* 19, 1960.

Welter, Erich. *Falsch und richtig planen. Eine kritische Studie über die deutsche Wirtschaftslenkung im zweiten Weltkrieg*. Heidelberg: Quelle und Meyer, 1954.

Winkel, Harald. "Die wirtschaftlichen Beziehungen Deutschlands zu Dänemark in den Jahren der Besetzung 1940–1945." In *Probleme der nationalsozialistischen Wirtschaftspolitik*. Edited by F. W. Henning. Berlin: Duncker und Humblot, 1976.

"Wirtschaftliche Aspekte des Anschlusses Österreichs an das Deutsche Reich: Ein Dokumentation." In *Militärgeschichtliche Mitteilungen* 2, 1970.

Wolfanger, Dieter. "Die nationalsozialistische Politik in Lothringen (1940–1945)." Dissertation, University of Saarbrücken, 1977.

———. *Nazification de la Lorraine mosellane.* Sarreguemines: Edition Pierron, 1982.

Zur Frage der Eisenerzversorgung Deutschlands, insbesondere Rheinland-Westfalens. In *Die Rohstoffversorgung der deutschen eisenerzeugenden Industrie. Verhandlungen und Berichte des Unterausschusses für Gewerbe: Industrie, Handel und Handwerk.* Edited by Ausschuß zur Untersuchung der Erzeugungs- und Absatzbedingungen der deutschen Wirtschaft (III. Unterausschuß). Berlin: E. S. Mittler und Sohn, 1928.

Index

Alsace, 9, 11–18, 48, 125n16
Arbed, 54, 66, 74
arms and munitions manufacturing and
spending, 32, 33, 34, 46, 47, 98, 111–14,
150n30, 153n60, 153n65
Aryanization campaigns: beneficiaries
of, 31; ethical and moral conduct of
Flick, 33, 41–42; Flick's involvement
in, 8, 25, 30–33, 37–42, 117, 132n25,
132n28, 136n79; Gau leadership policies and, 16; Hochofenwerk Lübeck,
25, 31, 37–38, 42; industrial community's opportunities through, 34; Keppler
Circle and, 30; Petschek family mine
operations, 25, 31, 38–42, 70, 134n59,
136n79; purpose of, 7, 23, 25; Simson/
Suhl venture, 31–33, 132n25, 132n28
Austria: Bürckel's administration of, 17;
German takeover of (Anschluss), 17,
40, 135n68; industry in, German takeover of, 20–21, 63; iron ore from, 45,
47; Petschek family mine operations,
40; U.S. and Germany relations and,
135n68
autarkic policies, 2, 3, 4–5, 46, 99, 118

Belgium, 22, 57–58, 64, 71, 138n29
Bismarckhütte, 27, 78, 82
Blitzkrieg economy, 3, 122n7
Bonnet, Georges, 13
Brenneke, Rudolf, 59
Briey, 21, 47, 73–74, 138n29
Brüning, Heinrich, 29
Bürckel, Josef: background and character
of, 15–16; labor and wage policy of,
109; Lorraine, administration of by,

15, 16–17, 23, 57, 58–59; Lorraine industry, distribution of to individuals, 82;
trustee arrangement, responsibility for
oversight of, 86, 92, 103
Burkart, Odilo: arms and munitions manufacturing, 112–13; Lorraine industry,
distribution of, 56, 70–71, 72, 73, 76;
private industry and Nazi regime policies, 92; Rombach, condition of, 102;
Rombach, interest in, 73, 78–79, 80;
trustee arrangements, 88, 89
Buskühl, Ernst, 66, 68–69

capitalism: authoritarian brand of, 33–34;
economic policies of Nazi regime, private industry, and, 20, 42, 91–92
Circle of Friends of Heinrich Himmler
(Keppler Circle), 25, 30, 38–39
coal and coke: coke, shortages of, 67, 97–99,
110–11, 144n16, 152n55; coke requirements for smelting, 145n30; distribution of Lorraine industries and supply
of, 74–76, 145n32; hard coal, 41; lignite
(brown coal), 38–39, 40, 41, 134n59,
134n61, 145n30; Reichswerke, coal
needs and resources, 41, 66–67, 81,
145n30; resources of German firms,
74–75, 145n30; Rombach, coke for, 65,
67–68, 78, 80, 81, 83, 84, 86, 97, 100–
101, 111, 143n11, 152n55
conservative elites and economic policies
of Nazi regime, 1–2
corporate community. See industrial
community
Czechoslovakia, 13, 20–21, 40, 45, 47, 63

policies, 15–16, 22–23, 32; industrial community, aid to, 4–5, 118; industrial community, collaboration with, 5–7; industrial community, relationship with, 1–2, 33–34; industrial community, support for from, 43–44; labor force policies, 107–8; military administration, 16–17, 18–19; occupation policy of, 1, 10; private industry and policies of, 20, 42, 91–92; rational means to pursue irrational ends, 118–19; seizure of power by, industrial community's role in, 5–7; Steinbrinck, connections to, 30; U.S., relations with, 135n68. *See also* Aryanization campaigns; economic policies of Nazi regime
Norway, 10, 47, 71

Petschek family mine operations, 25, 31, 38–42, 70, 134n59, 136n79
Pleiger, Paul, 34–35, 135n68
Poensgen, Ernst, 35, 51, 54, 55–56, 60, 73, 76, 80, 140n52, 142n77
Poland, 14, 21, 54

Raabe, Karl, 71–73, 76, 89, 101, 102, 146n54
Raabe, Paul, 21, 65, 129n60
rail system, deficiency of, 98–99, 149n12
Rauschning, Hermann, 12, 125n16
Reichert, Jacob Wilhelm, 56–57, 60, 71
Reichsvereinigung Eisen, 22
Reichswerke Hermann Göring: coal needs and resources, 41, 66–67, 81, 145n30; control and administration of industries by, 21–22, 33–34, 53–54, 63–64, 140n52; establishment of, 33–34, 35; expansion program of, 104; Flick, attitude of toward, 42; iron ore source for, 45, 99, 115; Lorraine industry, distribution of, 66, 69, 77, 144n15; opposition to and campaigns against, 35–36, 46; Rombach, bid for, 84; steel industry of, expansion of, 69–70; steel industry

operations and, 34–37, 134n46; success of, 45–46, 117
Rhein-Elbe-Union, 27–28
Ribbentrop, Joachim von, 13
Röchling, Hermann: administrative role in iron and steel industry, 21–22, 57–60, 65–66, 85, 86, 109; Flick, relationship with, 85, 146n47; labor force policies, 109; Lorraine industry, distribution of, 144n15; political and business prominence of, 58; Rombach, bid for, 84; Rombach, condition of, 101; Rombach, opposition to Flick's acquisition of, 84–85; steel plants of, French takeover of, 55–56, 58, 141n59
Rombach steel works: acquisition of by Flick, 1, 25, 143n5; acquisition of, formal memorandum for, 80–83; acquisition strategy, 70–83; advantages and drawbacks of, 65, 143nn9–11; appeal to Göring for acquisition of, 83, 145–46n43; assessment of suitability of, 72–73, 76–77; awarding of to Flick, 83–85, 146n45; coke for, sources for and transport of, 65, 67–68, 77, 78, 80, 81, 83, 84, 86, 97, 100–101, 111, 143n11, 152n55; condition of, 64–65, 72–73, 95, 101–3, 106, 142n4; establishment of, 1, 64; financing for purchase of, 68–69, 76; French takeover of, 64, 102, 143n6; furnaces and facilities, 64, 72, 104–5, 106, 113; German development and ownership of, 1, 64, 66, 80, 143n5, 144n15; Harpen mines and, 66–68, 69–70, 111, 114; Homecourt, partnership with, 77, 80–81, 143n9; inspection tour of, 102, 145–46n43; interest in and motive for acquiring, 61, 63, 66–70, 78–79, 80–83, 115–16, 142n77; investment in and renovation of, 102–5, 117, 150n27, 151n36; iron ore mines and extraction for, 64, 65, 143n7; labor force for, 77, 98, 106–10, 113, 152n48; location of, 1; long-term interest in,

ABOUT THE AUTHOR

Marcus Orin Jones is a history professor at the U.S. Naval Academy and a consultant for the Institute for Defense Analyses. He lives with his family in Cape St. Claire, Annapolis, Maryland.

The Naval Institute Press is the book-publishing arm of the U.S. Naval Institute, a private, nonprofit, membership society for sea service professionals and others who share an interest in naval and maritime affairs. Established in 1873 at the U.S. Naval Academy in Annapolis, Maryland, where its offices remain today, the Naval Institute has members worldwide.

Members of the Naval Institute support the education programs of the society and receive the influential monthly magazine *Proceedings* or the colorful bimonthly magazine *Naval History* and discounts on fine nautical prints and on ship and aircraft photos. They also have access to the transcripts of the Institute's Oral History Program and get discounted admission to any of the Institute-sponsored seminars offered around the country.

The Naval Institute's book-publishing program, begun in 1898 with basic guides to naval practices, has broadened its scope to include books of more general interest. Now the Naval Institute Press publishes about seventy titles each year, ranging from how-to books on boating and navigation to battle histories, biographies, ship and aircraft guides, and novels. Institute members receive significant discounts on the Press's more than eight hundred books in print.

Full-time students are eligible for special half-price membership rates. Life memberships are also available.

For a free catalog describing Naval Institute Press books currently available, and for further information about joining the U.S. Naval Institute, please write to:

Member Services
U.S. Naval Institute
291 Wood Road
Annapolis, MD 21402-5034
Telephone: (800) 233-8764
Fax: (410) 571-1703
Web address: www.usni.org